# THE DJEMBE GUIDI

## comment from users & teachers,

*".. I have had a good look through your book and I think it is excellent. You have done a rea.., j..,.. j.... .i, ana aiso with the Carabali CD. Can I order copies of both for the RNCM library ....."*

**Ian Wright** *(Director of Percussion Studies, Royal Northern College of Music, Manchester, UK)*

*".....I've been reading your book this week and wanted to say 'well done' - I think it is excellent...... I never realised it had such breadth..... it would take alot to surpass this as a beginner's book, and I reckon it's essential reading ...... I'll recommend it with conviction....."*

**Jon Dudley** *(Percusion Tutor, Leeds College of Music, Leeds, UK)*

*"...I have thoroughly enjoyed reading the book and listening to the CD........... I liked the scholarly introduction - it was informative, easy to read, and flowing...... You make useful comments and suggestions which will be of enormous help to those wishing to learn how to play the djembe........ I shall certainly use some of you ideas in my lectures, and will also advise students to puchase the book/CD........"*

**Caryl Roese** *(School of Education, Universtity of Wales Institute, Cardiff, Wales)*

*"..... I think you did a great job on the book: its obvious that you're a great teacher and that you really understand the beginner's mind. Betsy (Sansby - his co-author) and I both thought your writing was excellent....."*

**Alan Dworsky** *(Drum teacher and author of the award winning 'Conga Drumming')*

*".....The Djembe Guide ...is very well written and informative. An indication of the dedication of the author of any book is the depth of experience demonstrated, and the research into the subject matter - your book reflects these qualities to a high degree.... My friends who are into drumming think it is an excellent book, and recommend it to anyone wanting to know more about the djembe, its playing and its culture...."*

**John Bowden** *(Music teacher and author)*

## comments from retailers

*"..... Two thousand thanks ......the best book about djembe so far - recommended.... Bloody marvellous - send more !....."*

**Adaptatrap** *(Percussion shop - Brighton, UK)*

*"The Djembe Guide is the book we recommend to most djembe buyers - particularly if they don't read music, and it's been very well received...........The Carabali performance CD is a good idea for people to hear the rhythms in performance, with solo & improv, too............ a best seller because there's just so much in it .........."*

**Knock on Wood** *(Percussion shop - Leeds, UK)*

# THE DJEMBE GUIDE

# The Djembe Guide
## for beginners and intermediate groups

by Ianto Thornber

Published by
Need to Know (Music Publications)
14 Allerton Grange Vale
Leeds LS17 6LT  England
Email: ianto.thornber@virgin.net

ISBN  0-9538181-0-1

# Need to Know (Music Publications)
## Product Catalogue available at www.thedjembeguide.com

**The Djembe Guide**
Book/CD tutor pack
The Original Best Seller

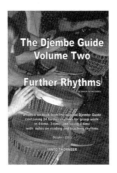

**The Djembe Guide Volume 2**
Book/CD tutor pack
Follow on for further group work

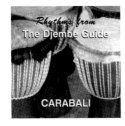

**Carabali: Rhythms from the Djembe Guide**
CD
West African style drumming

**BushGiants: Newlanding**
CD
Didjeridu Fusion

**An Introduction to the Boab Didjeridu**
Cassette
Didjeridu Tuition

# The Djembe Guide

About this book

The Djembe Guide is a resource book for anyone involved with the djembe, from novice players to the leaders and members of intermediate level groups.

The Djembe Guide assumes no prior knowledge of the djembe, or of music, but guides the reader carefully on a deliberate course of learning, from first steps and simple exercises, through easy patterns for small groups, and on to playing genuine West African multi-part rhythms in a drumming ensemble.

Rhythms and exercises are presented in a clear, easy to understand system, developed specifically for this book, combining elements of oral tradition and simple tablature, so you don't have to read musical score.

It includes chapters on the background to this fascinating drum, and it's recent rise to popularity outside the homelands of West Africa, and gives advice on finding, tuning and maintaining a drum of your own.

The Djembe Guide is the culmination of five trips to West Africa and more than twelve years drumming experience by the author, in community groups, performance groups, in public classes, and in education. With it's enclosed CD, simple tablature, and profuse illustrations, The Djembe Guide really works, to get you drumming, and is the next best thing to a personal tutor.

A NOTE FROM THE AUTHOR

This book has been several years in the making, and contains a learning programme distilled from all I have learned from other teachers, tempered by my own teaching experience. The presentation of rhythms in a three bar grid format is my own development, which we use successfully in groups I have taught. Your comments are most welcome, and the tuition programme contained in The Djembe Guide can hopefully develop and improve in future editions. Please send your written comments to me, care of the publisher. PLEASE DO NOT PHOTOCOPY THIS BOOK. If you wish to obtain quantities of The Djembe Guide for your group, please refer to your retailer or write to / email me.

Ianto Thornber  March 2000

# The Djembe Guide

## contents

# Dedication & Acknowledgments

I'd like to acknowledge and dedicate this book to all the people who have been instrumental in my own love affair with the djembe. It must have started whilst I've been working at Knock on Wood Multicultural Music Shop in Leeds, UK, and I should thank Andy Wilson, it's founder, for his infectious interest in all things musical - especially the more bizarre instruments from around the world. His skills and enthusiasm are still being spread through his workshops in schools and colleges in the UK.

coaxed me patiently into simple rhythms my brain and hands could cope with. Suddenly I was hooked.

Coming back to England, I took djembe lessons from Lamin Jassey in Leeds, and picked up more inspiration from Keith Jackman in York, and Roger Wolfe in Ilkley. Once you start looking, you tend to see things all around you that you didn't know were there before, and I began to find djembe enthusiasts all around Leeds. Particularly I'd like to mention Julian Marley, Anni and Paul of Drumcall, Dianne Vickers of Drumdance, the members of Janta Bi, and Tony Woods of Bradford Djembe Group.

Thanks also to Lorraine Coburn and Jesse Bannister, who taught me the dedication it takes to learn, and how to become 'immersed' in rhythm. My thanks also go to Barak Schmool, and the Senegalese drummer Magatte Djeng, who ran classes in Leeds through the winter of '97/'98, (honouring me with the chance to lead the class in one of his taught rhythms), and to Pierre La Blanche in South Africa, who taught me several of Jobina Pinkenburg's arrangements.

with Andy Wilson

It was on my second trip to Africa - specifically The Gambia - that I got my first experience of the djembe in the form of beach-side lessons from a drummer called King, who lived in Bakau, and played in a band called the Kunta Kinte Band around the bars and local hotels. It was from King and his band that I got a first hand experience of the live djembe played well, with the raw and raucous modern West African sound - a truly cross cultural mix of djembe, bougarabou, kora, trumpet, rakatak shakers and keyboard, played through an overstrained guitar amp. King's lessons in the beach bar were the first time I felt I might be able to play the drum, as he

In much of my own teaching I have used rhythms learned from tuition videos by Paulo Mattioli, Brad Dutz, and Jim Greiner, and other rhythms picked up at groups in England, West Africa & South Africa. I must thank anyone who has been to my classes for their attention and support. I hope we have allowed each other the freedom to make mistakes without criticism, and aided each other's learning. Also thanks to the members of 'Carabali' - a performance group which has gradually grown out of the classes.

(iv)

Special thanks to John Dudley and David Ledsam for their enthusiasm and support, and to my partner Jo and daughter Holly, who have done without me for the many hours of research, compilation and writing of this book. Also Lindsay, Sarah and See Ken Pang for type setting and editing.

I must also thank the suppliers of the many djembes which we have supplied through Knock on Wood, these being Michael Rottger, Lamin Jassey, Claude Adjanahoun, Abdul Ngom and Mark Hutchison, Sekou Keita and Tata Bah (who also let me watch, discuss, and photograph the building process step by step), and of course, King, who supplied my own djembe, amongst many.

The following authors (of books, articles, and internet pages) I also acknowledge and thank - their works all precede mine:

• Mark Sunkett for 'Mandiani Drum and Dance'

• Serge Blanc for 'African Percussion -The Djembe'

• James River Drums for their internet site notes

• Eric Charry for 'A guide to the Djembe' (article for 'Percussive Notes' Vol 34, No2

• Rosemary Schonfeld for 'Drumatrix'

• Arthur Hull for 'Drum Circle Spirit'

• David Locke for 'Drum Gahu'

Jon Dudley

with Arthur Hull

# Part One

## Background

# What is a Djembe?

What's all the fuss about? What's so special about the djembe (pronounced 'JEMBAY') that there are so many new players all the time, and djembe groups all over the country are filling up and branching out. Ten or fifteen years ago you'd have been hard pressed to find anyone who'd even heard of this drum in the UK, and numerous percussion books from before the 1990s don't even mention it, yet now, in 1999 there are at least three annual festivals which are practically dedicated to it, and others which feature it strongly in their teaching programme.

The djembe has blossomed out from its roots in the West African Mande homelands of what is now Guinea and southern Senegal since the first visits to the USA by Les Ballets Africains in the 1950s, and is now the first choice for many aspiring hand drummers throughout the Western world. More on this later - but what exactly is a djembe?

The djembe is a goblet shaped drum which is open at the base, and has a single head stretched over the top. An average or 'standard' djembe might be between 45 and 65 cm tall, with a head diameter of 25 to 35 cm, but a wide range of sizes can be found, from tiny drums best suited to children, through to monster djembes which have to be supported on stands to be played. The shape is reminiscent of the North African darabukas and dumbeks, but these drums are typically smaller (for playing on the lap) and made from clay or metal, whereas the typical African djembe is of wood. Traditionally the wooden body was carved from a single piece of tree trunk, with certain types of wood (eg Lingue, Mango, Iroca) being favoured in different regions. A goat or antelope hide is stretched tightly over the top of the body, and held clamped between two metal rings. Rope runs from these top rings to a third ring at the waist of the drum, and this is commonly tightened by a method known as the 'Mali Weave' to achieve the desired tuning. (For tuning details, see chapter 11).

The beauty of the djembe, and what attracts most people to it, I believe, is the sound, or rather the range of sounds which can be produced from it. A well tuned djembe has a deep, resonant bass, a tight edge tone and a superb, sharp slap which puts many other drums to shame. It's easy to learn these tones (see chapter 4 for details) and to produce simple yet mesmeric rhythms which can be layered one on top of another to great effect. At its most basic it's great fun, and as you become more involved in the rhythms you are led into

a greater understanding not only of music, but also of Africa, and many players end up visiting the djembe in its traditional home.

Shops these days also stock modern versions of the djembe which are made by big drum companies such as LP, Remo, Afro, Meinl, CP, Headliner, Toca, and some independents, like Natal. Most of these have a body built from staves like a conga (or a beer barrel), but in the djembe shape, and often you can choose from standard sizes. Most of the western djembes have 'nut & bolt' style lug tuning, but a few manufacturers offer rope tuning either as standard, (eg Natal) or optional (eg Remo). The djembe has become popular in other African countries, and are now made in some quantity in Ghana and South Africa. Djembes are also made in certain parts of Asia, notably Indonesia and similar drums in the Canary Isles and Balearics from Palm tree stumps.

Whether you fancy an African or Western style drum, don't buy until you have read chapter 10, which gives you tips on what to look for -and look out for - and how to get the right size drum for your personal physique and likely usage.

## Structure, Size and Pitch

Any experience of djembes in a group will soon convince you that different drums have different sounds - these differences are created by the individual shape of each drum, and by how it is tuned. Two drums side by side, which are tuned to sound their best, will still sound different from each other, due to differences in the shapes and sizes of the different parts - the bowl and the stem. Studies have been done which show that the interior shape of the bowl affects the pitch of the open tone, and the depth and curve at the base of the bowl affects the reflected pitch of the slap tone. The overall length of the whole drum will determine the low bass tone, and the size of the interior hole, and slope of the stem walls will affect

the bass resonance, giving a higher resonance with greater flare.

Having said all that, what most people want to know is how to find a drum with either lots of bass, or with a good sharp slap tone. As a rule of thumb, with all other things being equal, a taller drum should give you lower bass, a flared stem should give you a bigger sounding bass, and a smaller bowl should give you a higher tone and stronger slap, but other things are never equal in the world of hand made instruments, and you will find that other factors such as the skin, the wood thickness and the tightness of tuning confusing the above theories. It has been noted by one author that whilst in present day Guinea the djembes are small headed, with more cylindrical stems and a shallower bowl (less emphasis on bass), Malian drums have larger head diameter, deeper bowls, and longer stems, and Senegalese drums fall between the two extremes, and it is possible to hear the difference in the music produced by groups from these respective places.

## Accessories and Add Ons

The majority of Western players use their drums in groups, often sitting in a circle on chairs with their drums between their

knees, and with the possible exception of a waist strap, there is nothing else you need to play your drum. If you have an African djembe with rope tuning you will need some basic knowledge of the 'Mali weave' tuning system to keep your drum in fine fettle, and it's also a good idea to get some kind of cover if you intend to move you drum from place to place. These come in the form of cloth bags, padded head covers, padded carrying bags and semi-stiff plastic drum cases. You need to see your local drum shop to decide which type is best for you - greater cover obviously equals greater protection, and you should also consider

your (quite heavy) drum causing damage to other things, say, in the car boot, if it has no padding around it.

Some djembe players prefer to stand whilst playing, using either a drum stand or a shoulder strap (see chapter 4 for descriptions of these), and some tie on or otherwise attach rattles of various descriptions, which give a little jingle whilst the drum is being played. These can be very attractive, but are entirely optional, and you can choose to personalise your drum in this way, or not, as you see fit.

# The Djembe in Africa

To many people in the west, the djembe is the quintessential 'African drum'. Of course, the djembe is not the only African drum - far from it - but it is the one that people come across most often. Other common African drums include the Nigerian 'dondo' talking drum, the smaller Senegambian 'tama' talking drum, Ghanaian kpanlogo and agbadza sets (which each include a range of sizes and shapes in their ensembles), original Yoruba 'bata' drums from Nigeria, which are now better known as the voudou drum of the Cuban Santeria religion, and other drums superficially similar to the djembe - 'sabarr', 'sourouba', 'bougarabou' and 'goumbe'. The djembe itself is usually accompanied by cylindrical bass drums known as the 'djundjun' (individually, the 'djun djun', 'sangbani', and 'kenkeni'). These are all drums to be found in the West African bulge countries which were part of the great Mali Empire when it spread from the Sahara desert to the Niger river between 1000AD and 1500AD.

## MANINKA- MALINKA- MANDINKA

Maninka, Malinka and Mandinka are cultural names which will always be associated with the peoples of West Africa. To avoid confusion, it's worth noting the following : The homeland of the Maninka people is/was called Mande. 'Mali' is said to be a re-formation of the word 'Mande', and the words 'Maninka', 'Malinka', and 'Mandinka' are all used to describe peoples of the same cultural group. Further subdivisions can be found in the vernacular of local people - for instance the Maninka from the region of Caron can be called Caroninka. This is an area where the novice must tread carefully, as it is possible to cause insult to someone West African by alluding to their family

history or regionality without care. The Susu (or Soso) are/were close relatives of the Maninka from further north in what is now the modern state of Mali. Confusions can easily arise with unfamiliar names, and different spellings are often found for the same words due to the phonetic translations from African local dialects to European languages. Also there are differences between the modern state borders and the cultural or tribal borders both ancient and modern.

## NUMU, JELI AND GRIOT

Whilst there are differences in the oral histories regarding the origin of the djembe, we can be fairly certain that it arose in the area between the Faranah region of Guinea, Bamako (in present day Mali), and Tambacounda (in modern Senegal), amongst the people known as the Malinka. In Guinea, one oral history

Kora player on the Gambia river

has it that the Malinka people migrated to the area in the 9th century. The Diula (of Mali) were known as trades people, and may have been instrumental in the spread of the drum throughout the empire in the following years. Another story is that the drums were built by a class of hereditary professional blacksmiths of Malinka/Susu origin called Numu. Three great 'Numu' family names - Camara, Doumbia, and Kante, are known to this day amongst djembe aficionados. It's worth noting, however, that the Numu were/are not the hereditary professional musicians of West Africa - that position belongs to the 'Djeli/Jeli' families (whom the French

Balafon player

called 'Griots') - most notably the Kouyate and Diabate families. Their instruments are primarily the kora, the balafon, and the koni, and their lifestyle differed from the Numu in that they were musical artisans, (often compared to the wandering minstrels of old Europe, and probably quite dependent on the patronage of the noble 'Horon' families such as the Keita, Konate, Kone & Traore), whereas the Numu were primarily village based crafts people. The role of the Jeli was to play and sing about events and people either in court or in the village, whereas the role of the Numu was to make things and play drums for dancing at events in the village. Some modern djembe players have Malinka Horon names, (eg Mamady Keita), and many have Numu names, but it's rare to find a djembe player with a Jeli name.

Thus, the homelands of the djembe in Africa are the originating areas of Guinea, Mali and Senegal, along with the bordering countries of Ivory Coast, The Gambia, and Burkina Faso. Although the drums are also now made in elsewhere in Western Africa, the greatest skill and knowledge remains in the original countries.

## DRUM AND DANCE

There are regional differences in the appearance and tone of djembes from different areas (see chapter 1) but the general usage of the drum would be fairly consistent, in that the djembe is an instrument from an ensemble of drums & percussion which also contains the cylindrical djundjun in three sizes, iron bells of different shapes (which are often attached to the djundjun), gourd or basket rattles, and often other hand percussion. In addition to the musicians there will be dancers in a troupe, and the dancers and percussionists may swap roles.

The bass drums (djundjun) will play a melodic pattern between themselves, and this is overlaid by two or more basic djembe parts, with accompanying hand percussion - shakers, bells, wood blocks, gourd or basket rattles, and on top of all this will be one or more djembe soloists who will rotate or pass the solo part amongst themselves.

When not playing solo, a soloist will join one of the other djembe parts. The eyes of the ensemble are on the dancers, because the relationship between the dancing and the drumming is very close. The language of the djembe can call out a particular dancer to the floor, and the tempo of the rhythm can be altered to suit different people. (There is a big difference between playing in a village setting, for people of all ages in the village to dance, and playing in a performance situation with a pre-determined dance routine carried out by a rehearsing dance troupe - a bit like the difference between European folk musicians playing for a village hall ceilidh, compared to a Morris dance band, who play for their own dancers).

## DJEMBEFOLA

In Guinea, a djembe master is called a 'djembefola', and in all likelihood, he will have been dedicated to the drum since a very early age. In the film 'Djembefola', the Guinean master Mamady Keita is shown visiting his home village and his old masters after spending twenty six years abroad. In the village drum school, there are boys five or six years old who play djembe very well - Keita himself was good enough by the age of seven to play in a film called 'African Dance' which starred Harry Belafonte, and by the time he was fourteen he was selected to play in the National Ballet Djoliba.

Any culture produces it's own prodigies, of course, so we should not be suprised that in a culture where the djembe ensemble (read 'orchestra') is the main vehicle of musical expression, masters of that vehicle are produced.

One aspect of African life, which many Westerners are unaware of, is the different attitude towards time - we are all too often ready to give up trying to do something after only a few minutes of failure, when an hour of steady effort might produce the result we're looking for. Perhaps this is because we are so often labouring alone, as we have been taught to do our best, on our own, without help, whereas in African society, one is very rarely on one's own, help is usually at hand, and time is not something which feels rushed.

King with a young pupil

# The Djembe Leaves Africa

## AN HISTORICAL PERSPECTIVE

Musicians in the 1950s were used to the Latin sounds of son, rhumba and mambo which came from Cuba, and turned into salsa in New York. Drummers knew the congas, bongos and timbales, but never really heard the djembe until 'Les Ballets Africains', from Guinea, began to tour the world.

In Guinea, between the 1950s and the 1980s, President Toure funded the arts very well, whilst not encouraging the interest of foreigners in his country. At the end of his office, funding for the arts declined, and drummers began to find that there was an interest in their music in other countries.

In the USA, interest centred around the Guinean, Ladji Camara, and in Europe, Mamady Keita and Famadou Konate came to stay and teach. Since then, the 'world music' boom has created a tidal wave of enthusiasts for this 'new' drum, which is considered by many to be the most popular drum in the world today.

## OPENING THE VILLAGE CIRCLE

There have been many effects of the arrival of the djembe outside the traditional African village setting.Perhaps the first one is the most symbolic - the village circle with dancers in the middle was opened out to become a line across a stage, with choreographed dancers across the front. This was obviously necessary to make a stage show, and without those shows, many of us would never have encountered the djembe, but we must be aware that staged presentation for a seated, non - participating, audience was a significant change in the usage of the drum. The biggest change was in the interaction between the drummers and the dancers - since the dancing was planned and choreographed in advance, the role of the drum language became merely to signal, rather than to talk.

## DRUMMING TO WESTERN EARS

Something else happened when Western musical minds heard the African rhythms, and began to wonder how to write them down. The oral teaching tradition of Africa came face to face with the written teaching tradition of the West. It was obvious to Westerners that the drums were played like an orchestra, and they were excited enough by the performances to want to learn to play, but the Western penchant for standardisation has led to difficulties.

For a start, in the West, all the members of an orchestra have to play in the same rhythm, otherwise the conductor gets very upset, but in African drumming, the use of polyrhythm - (more than one rhythm at the same time) is as common as the use of harmony - (more than one note at the same time) is in the West. This has been an exciting and unusual challenge for most Western musicians, and is part of the great lure of drumming as a whole.

## STANDARDISATION?

Also, we have a liking in the West for things to stay the same once we have written them down, otherwise it may not be worth writing them down and claiming our authorship in the first place, but we have mis-interpreted the way the African rhythms are formed, and we have sometimes ended up arguing about (for instance) whether a particular djembe part comes from one rhythm or another one, when in the original form, it is the djun-djun playing which defines the rhythm, not the djembe parts at all! One author claims that there are really only a handful of variations in djembe parts, and all the rest represent minor changes on the basic few - which is a bit like the claim that there are only really a handful of stories to be told, and all the books ever written are simply variations and updates on the same themes.

In Africa, the non-standardised use of the drum, and the oral teaching method, leads to many variations in any one rhythm, and there are different local names for similar rhythms in different regions. Even specific village rhythms vary slowly over time, as the drum language evolves with normal use. Beware the drummer who thinks he knows it all - African or European!

## LEARNING THE LINGO

Someone once wrote that it's ironic that a drum which has a voice and language like that of the djembe so often speaks to those that do not understand it, and when they themselves play it, there is no-one who understands it listening. They were, of course, referring to the legions of djembe lovers who listen to the drum but do not hear what would originally have been heard in the same rhythms when they were played in the village setting, and when they play the drum away from the village setting, there

Bakau schoolchildren

is no-one to listen to and respond to what they are playing - even if they get it right!

It would be a task of many years to really get to know the language of the djembe, and most of us who are learning may never get to become fluent. We are too far removed from the original culture and situation to gain anything but the most basic understanding of drum language, but by going to Africa we can at least get to see the drum in something like it's original setting, and that can be a very moving experience for anyone.

At a Moslem school in Bakau in the Gambia I once heard a class of children - more used to reciting the Koran by heart - suddenly switch to reciting the song 'Old Macdonald had a farm', for my benefit, without the faintest idea of what they were saying - and that night at my djembe class I realised I was doing exactly the same thing with my drum language! The novice European djembe drummer often plays by rote, duplicating as closely as possible what he or she has heard, but often playing with a thick, 4/4 rock'n'roll accent, struggling like a Yorkshireman at a French evening class.

## OUT OF AFRICA
## - HOW THE DJEMBE HAS CHANGED

Because manufacturing conditions in Africa often, to our eyes, leave a lot to be desired, many of the drums made are what a Westerner might call 'eccentric', and as a market for the drum has developed worldwide, so the range of quality of African sourced drums has increased, and it's now possible to buy a really bad African djembe, as well as a good one. At the same time, some African suppliers (particularly in Ivory Coast) have realised that there is a large income available from the West, and have changed their techniques to produce a more westernised product which has greater appeal outside West Africa.

Once the djembe became recognised outside of Africa, and people started buying them in quantities, some of the larger drum manufacturers in the West began to make their own versions for the Western market. Many produce their 'djembes' in the same way that they make their congas, by constructing the body either from fibreglass, or from staves like a barrel, and then attaching a pre-formed head by means of a metal ring and tuning lugs which attach to the body via brackets. The lug & bracket system does away with the need to understand the 'Mali weave' rope tuning system, because it does away with

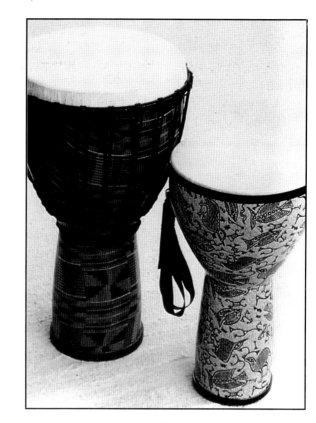

These American djembes are totally synthetic, and 100% vegan

ropes altogether, but one or two makers have recognised that this use of large bolt and bracket assemblies is difficult for the average player to hold between the knees when they are seated, and they have reverted back to the use of rope tuning. Of course, nut and bolt head attachment has the advantage that a broken head can be changed very quickly - a great advantage for professional drummers on the road.

Another major innovation has been the development of synthetic djembe heads which do not react to heat, cold or humidity - the latest generation of these heads give a superb performance, and can be tuned to sound as good as the best goatskins.

# Part Two

Beginning to drum

# Playing Positions & Basic Strokes For Djembe

This chapter is to show you how to hold your djembe or strap it on, and play some of the many sounds which are available from it.

## PLAYING SITTING DOWN

This is probably the most common position for playing the djembe, as it is the position used by most drumming groups and circles in this country and abroad. It's important to have the right size drum if you are to play sitting down. (See 'getting the right size drum' in chapter 10).

Sit on the front edge of an average size chair, and grip the drum between your knees (or cross your legs around it) whilst leaning it away from you so that the base of the drum is open. It's important that the base is open to let the sound out at the bottom, and the playing edge of the drum needs to be a few inches above the level of your thigh. Too low, and you can't reach some of the positions. Too high, and you will get tired as you play with your shoulders lifted up.

Hold the base of your drum between your feet if you wish - this can help the connection between your body and the drum, and help to stabilise it, but try not to lift the drum off the floor with your knees or your feet. The reason is that when you hit the drum, it may bounce down against the floor, which can cause cracks in the base.

Try to play with your back straight, but don't get all stiff - it's important to stay relaxed. This can be quite a challenge if you've not done much drumming before, because it's quite hard work, and can be tiring. Playing with a straight back can help you to play for longer without getting the aches and pains which can plague all players, old and new.

## PLAYING WITH YOUR DRUM STRAPPED ON

Standing up with the drum strapped on is the preferred method for many players on stage, and for many teachers in drum circles. Obviously this gives you freedom to move around whilst playing, however, it is more tiring and you need to be even more careful of your posture because you are not only carrying the weight of the drum, you are also exerting pressures on your own shoulders when playing the drum, yet your shoulders need to stay flexible and free moving to play properly!

For these reasons, you should only play standing up if you have to, when you are a beginner, though it would be worth it to learn how to put the drum on, just for

**23**

the experience. Read how to attach a strap at the end of chapter 5. You will soon get a feel for the length of the strap by your comfort level when playing the various strokes. If the strap is too long, you won't be able to reach down for the proper bass note. Too short, and your arms will feel hampered and your shoulders will rise when you play edge tones. Really the position is entirely up to you, and is based on where the drum feels comfortable to you.

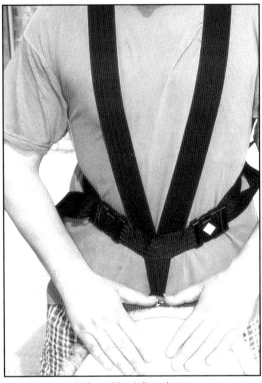
playing with a 'clip on' strap

The size of the drum is not important when you play standing up, because it does not stand between your knees, and the 'height above your thighs' is not relevant - but there must be very few drums which are ONLY ever played standing, and never sitting down.

You may occasionally see djembe players who are wearing the drum on a strap or waistband, and are playing bent over almost so they could touch their toes. I don't know anyone who plays like this for fun, but I have seen people play with neither strap nor chair and who therefore lie the drum on the floor and bend over it or sit on it to play.

## DJEMBE STANDS

Several types of djembe stand are available which will hold the drum up off the floor for you at the correct angle for playing, so that, if you don't want to wear the drum on a strap, you can put it on a stand, and (for instance) leave it on the stage whilst you go off and play your keyboard. There are brand name stands available from Gibraltar, Toca, LP, Pulse and Natal, which all vary slightly in design. I would recommend trying out any stand in-store, as the different designs allow different adjustments to be made to the position the drum is held, and if you have an African djembe, rather than a branded one, it may not fit on some stands. The thickness of the wood at the drum base is often important here.

Djembe on Gibraltar stand

# BASIC STROKES FOR THE DJEMBE

The djembe skin can be hit in lots of ways, in lots of positions, with different parts of the hand, or with a stick. In music, there are few hard and fast rules, and if you can make it work, it's OK, even if no-one has ever done it before. You can strike the skin of your drum in any way, and get a reasonable tone - my intention is to guide you into playing a simple scale of clear, distinct tones which you can quickly memorise and reproduce at will, and, most importantly, play without hurting your hands. The system I use is the Yoruba basic scale GUN/ DUN, GO/ DO, PA/TA (for bass, tone and slap). This is a rising scale of 'notes' which you can practice like any other musician would practice, following the exercises in the next chapter. This system was popularised in the West by Arthur Hull, following the teaching of the Nigerian, Babatunde Olatunji in the USA.

## THE BASS TONES - GUN & DUN

 CD 1

The bass stroke is played with a hand at, or near, the centre of the drum. The idea is to bounce your whole hand off the skin without too much slapping sound, and the tone will come out of the bottom of the drum, to make the air around you go BOOM. You don't have to hit the skin very hard - just bounce your hand so that the drumskin is left vibrating freely. The whole of your hand should be inside the rim of the drum, and the hand should have some small degree of firmness to it - not loose and floppy, but not stiff either. Experiment till you get the right sound, and listen to the example on the tape/CD.

The right hand bass note is called GUN, and the left is called DUN. You may find that one hand is easier to control than the other when you first begin, but eventually, after some practise, you can make both GUN and DUN sound the same. Let your better hand 'teach' the other one what to do.

Only one hand should be on the skin at a time. If the second hand is on the skin, then the skin will not vibrate freely as it should for GUN & DUN.

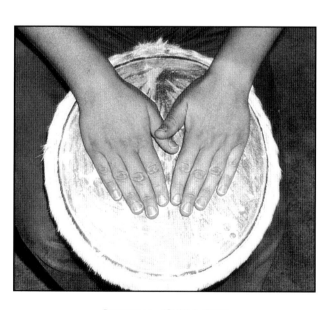

Bass tones - 'GUN' & 'DUN'

Right hand bass - 'GUN'

## THE EDGE TONES - GO & DO

 CD 1

The edge tones (sometimes just called 'tones') are played at the edge of the drum -suprisingly! Move your hands backwards towards you from the GUN/DUN position, until the knuckle at the base of your finger line has come off the edge of the drum. The pads of your four fingers are now on the drumskin, but the knuckles are off the edge. When you bounce your hand off the drum it is the pads of your whole fingers which strike the skin. The fingers are firm but not tense, and loosely held together.

The right hand stroke is called GO, and the left hand, DO.

You will find that you can play these tones quite 'closed' and 'flat' - by making your fingers flat on the skin, or quite 'open' and 'ringy' by playing with your fingers at more of an angle.

These are the extremes of the GO/DO stroke, but unless the rhythm calls for one extreme or the other, you can play GO and DO midway between the extremes.

Listen to the examples on the tape / CD, and try to get the right and left hands to sound the same, as with the bass strokes.

## HAND CARE TIPS FOR GO / DO

You really need to look after your hands if you want to advance in drumming - bruises on the hands can be very off-putting. Keep the effort light, and concentrate on getting the right positions for your hands. In GO / DO your thumbs can be kept away from the edge of the drum by pointing them at each other (see photo). It is important to think about your thumb position because if you don't keep them out of the way, they can quickly get bruised on the drum edge.

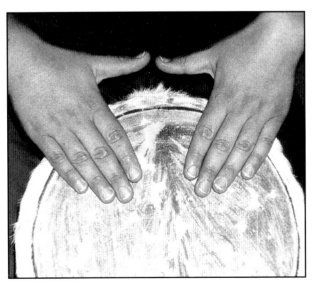

Edge tones - 'GO' & 'DO'

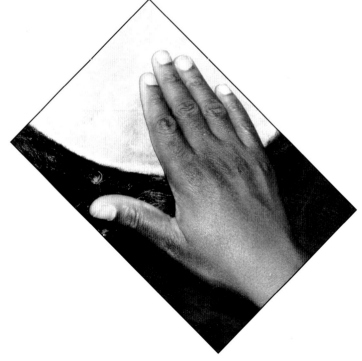

Right hand tone - 'GO'

## THE SLAP TONES - PA & TA

 **CD 1**

The slap tone has elements of both the previous tones in its sound. It's quite bright and strong, but not really ringy, it has a little bass, but does not boom. It's played near the edge of the drum, with the knuckle line over the edge onto the playing surface, and the hand relaxed a bit so that a space forms underneath the palm. The fingertips almost reach to the middle of the drum, and the edge of the drum is under the palm, from the base of the thumb to the base of the little finger. The elbows are fairly low, the wrists quite relaxed, and the hand is bounced off the drum skin so that the fingertip pads flick quite sharply on and off the surface with a slap. The slight hollow under the palm gives the tone a 'hollow' cupped sound, whilst the flicking action provides the characteristic sharpness, and the reach of the fingertips towards the middle gives the tone its bass depth.

The right hand stroke is called PA, and the left hand, TA.

Listen to the examples, and practice lightly on your drum, concentrating on the hand position. As with other strokes, try to get the right and left to sound the same.

## HAND CARE FOR PA / TA

It's very tempting to try to play PA & TA by striking hard at the drum in the hope that strength will produce the correct tones, but the usual result of that approach is sore hands and a discouraged player. It can take some time to get this tone right at first, and although the slap tones CAN be very loud, it is not the volume which makes the tone, but the hand position, and it's better to take care and practice with less effort at first, so that later the strength of the tone can be increased safely.

You should expect your fingertips to sting a little when you slap on your drum, just as they would if you slapped your own thigh, (or anything else, for that matter). The thumb position is very important in PA / TA because the flicking motion can easily produce bruises when practicing - lift the thumb slightly to avoid hurting it. Also, it's important to make sure that the big pads at the base of the hand are taking the brunt of the strike, rather than the middle of the palm. If you hit the middle of the palm repeatedly on the drum edge, you are very likely to get bruising between the thumb and the first finger. You can avoid this by making sure that the whole of the thumb is over the drumskin, and pointing forward.

Slap tones - 'Pa' & 'Ta'

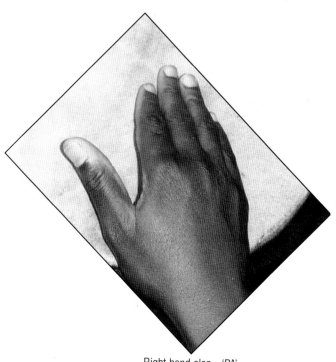

Right hand slap - 'PA'

# Practice Rhythms & Exercises For Djembe

Now you know the three basic strokes, it's time to learn some exercises to help you actually play the drum. The aim of these exercises is to give you the ability to play the strokes both accurately and 'fluently'. This is the way to become a more 'musical' drummer - remember the strokes must be heard to be different from one another - the sounds of Gun/Dun, Go/Do and Pa/Ta should be easy for a listener to distinguish as you play and practice.

It's a good idea to start slowly on any exercise or new rhythm - any musician will tell you that. If you rush at things, you may find yourself doing them quickly but wrongly, and doing it wrong in hand drumming can quickly lead to bruised hands.

"Practice slow - learn quick!"

It's also a good idea to recognise that you probably have a strong hand and a not-so-strong hand. I have assumed that you are using your right hand for Gun, Go, and Pa, but if your strong hand is your left, you can use your left hand for these strokes. It won't make any difference to your ability to play, and I hope the exercises and rhythms laid out in this book will be easy for all to follow.

**TEN STEPS TO GOOD DRUMMING**

**1. Drumming regularly -**
a bit of practice regularly will get you further, faster, than a lot of practice occasionally.

**2. Developing stamina -**
you will need to be able to keep going when you get tired, to keep up with a group.

**3. Waking up your sleepy hand -**
practice using your 'other' hand until it becomes as active and strong as your 'strong' hand - a good trick is to try getting up in the morning, get dressed, clean your teeth etc, using your 'other' hand.

**4. Learning the basic hand positions -**
really get to know those hand positions - it's the only way to play comfortably.

**5. Playing the basic strokes with clarity -**
when you develop clarity between the strokes, and can move between them with ease, you really begin to sound like a drummer.

**6. Learning some rhythm parts -**
now you're cookin', your drumming
starts to sound more expressive, and
you recognise different ways of counting
the background structures.

**7. Getting to know complementary
rhythm parts -**
you get to feel how rhythm parts fit
together, and get involved in group
drumming.

**8. Learning complex, multi- part
rhythms -**
becoming a team player is now para-
mount, as you become able to listen to
many parts at once, and play your part
without distraction.

**9. Supporting the group leader/soloist -**
doing all the above in performance
situation, listening for signals, playing
breaks, and coping with rhythmic shifts.

**10. Learning to play improvisation
and solo -**
many people wish this was the first step,
but it really depends on the above steps
being in place.

# PRESENTATION OF EXERCISES AND RHYTHMS

The basic strokes are presented here like a scale from low (Gun/Dun) through middle (Go/Do) to high (Pa/Ta). Therefore they can be written on a kind of ladder just like any musical scale, and the scale or ladder has three steps to signify low, middle or high:

Pa & Ta_____

Go & Do_____

Gun & Dun_____

As you read the whole scale (all three lines) from left to right, you can see quickly and easily which tone to play, from its low, middle or high position.

## TIMING
Next we have to give an idea of the timing of the exercise. Dividing the scale above with vertical lines at equal intervals gives an idea of timing. Each vertical line represents an equal amount of time passing, and with this improvement you can now read where there might be any gaps in the rhythm.

## INFLECTION
This simple system tells you the basics of the timing, but it doesn't tell you the inflection, or 'swing' of a rhythm. To really feel the swing of a rhythm, listen to the examples on the CD, as you read the rhythm on the page.

## GHOSTING
Ghosting is a technique used by drummers to help them make gaps of the right length in the rhythms they play. What you do is, you move your hand as if you were going to hit the drum, but you don't actually play any stroke - this means you can keep your hands moving at the same speed all the time, and the gaps in the rhythm can be defined in length by the number of 'ghost' strokes. Ghost strokes in our scale would appear as a time slot where no stroke is written in the low, middle, or high box, and there should be no sound at that point.

⌐Rpt.

| | | | Pa | Ta | | | | | | Pa | Ta | |
|---|---|---|---|---|---|---|---|---|---|---|---|---|
| | | Go | Do | | | | | Go | Do | | | |
| Gun | Dun | | | | | | Gun | Dun | | | | |

**SAY IT BEFORE YOU PLAY IT**

You can now read the scale, and see what will happen and when, and you can say, or sing the rhythm part to yourself before you play it, and whilst you practice it. Singing it to yourself helps you to internalise the part, and gets you into the swing of what is going to happen, before you actually do it. Remember always to take your time, and don't hurry yourself.

# EXERCISE ONE  CD 2

This exercise simply repeats the basic pairs of strokes over and over again, without any ghost strokes

|  |  |  |  | Pa | Ta | Rpt. |  |  |  | Pa | Ta |
|---|---|---|---|---|---|---|---|---|---|---|---|
|  | Go | Do |  |  |  |  | Go | Do |  |  |  |
| Gun | Dun |  |  |  | Gun | Dun |  |  |  |  |  |

# EXERCISE TWO  CD 2

This one adds a little spice by changing the order of the pairs

|  |  |  |  | Pa | Ta |  | Pa | Ta |  |  | Rpt. |
|---|---|---|---|---|---|---|---|---|---|---|---|
|  | Go | Do |  |  | Go | Do |  |  |  |  |  |
| Gun | Dun |  |  |  |  |  |  |  | Gun | Dun |  |

Notice that the cycle of six pairs both starts and ends on Gun Dun, so you have to play Gun Dun twice, when you repeat the cycle.

# EXERCISE THREE

You can make this exercise up yourself by changing the order of the pairs any way you want to. Try to keep the clarity between the strokes, and keep the tempo (speed) steady.

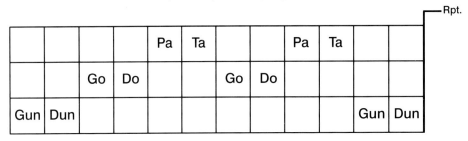

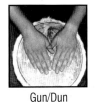
Gun/Dun

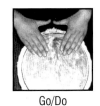
Go/Do

Pa/Ta

# EXERCISES FOUR, FIVE & SIX  CD 3

These three exercises help you practice moving from one stroke to the other two strokes.

**Exercise Four** — Rpt. (repeat from column 7)

| | | Pa | Ta | | | | | | | Pa | Ta | | | | |
|---|---|---|---|---|---|---|---|---|---|---|---|---|---|---|---|
| Go | Do | | | Go | Do | | | Go | Do | | | Go | Do | | |
| | | | | | | Gun | Dun | | | | | | | Gun | Dun |

**Exercise Five** — Rpt. (repeat from column 7)

| Pa | Ta | | | Pa | Ta | | | Pa | Ta | | | Pa | Ta | | |
|---|---|---|---|---|---|---|---|---|---|---|---|---|---|---|---|
| | | Go | Do | | | | | | | Go | Do | | | | |
| | | | | | | Gun | Dun | | | | | | | Gun | Dun |

**Exercise Six** — Rpt. (repeat from column 7)

| | | Pa | Ta | | | | | | | Pa | Ta | | | | |
|---|---|---|---|---|---|---|---|---|---|---|---|---|---|---|---|
| | | | | | | Go | Do | | | | | | | Go | Do |
| Gun | Dun | | | Gun | Dun | | | Gun | Dun | | | Gun | Dun | | |

# EXERCISE SEVEN

Now practice the pairs in greater numbers before changing smoothly to a different pair eg ten pairs of Go Do followed by ten pairs of Gun Dun followed by ten pairs of Pa Ta, and vary the number of pairs and the order you follow to your own choice.

As a break from playing just a right hand / left hand pair in each position, you can try playing three strokes in each position instead of two - it's quite tricky at first, but a very good exercise.

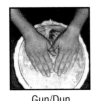
Gun/Dun

Go/Do

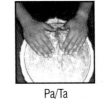
Pa/Ta

# EXERCISE EIGHT    CD 4

## BREAKING AWAY FROM PAIRS

'Real' parts will be a mixture of single strokes, ghost strokes, pairs of strokes, triplets, quads etc, so you will not always be playing both hands at the same position. If you did, the music would sound pretty restricted. Most people really have to work at 'waking up' their 'not-so-strong' hand to break away from stroke pairs and still play fluently. It's quite hard at first to get your weak hand to do what you want it to do (especially at the right time), but if you persevere, you can wake it up, and get it to respond just as well as your strong hand.

Rpt.

| Pa | | | | | Ta | | | Pa | | | | | Ta | | |
|---|---|---|---|---|---|---|---|---|---|---|---|---|---|---|---|
| | Do | Go | Do | Go | | Go | Do | | Do | Go | Do | Go | | Go | Do |
| | | | | | | | | | | | | | | | |

# EXERCISE NINE    CD 4

This is a variation of the above, with the Ta strokes replaced by Dun strokes, just to get that hand up to speed!

Rpt.

| Pa | | | | | | | | Pa | | | | | | | |
|---|---|---|---|---|---|---|---|---|---|---|---|---|---|---|---|
| | Do | Go | Do | Go | | Go | Do | | Do | Go | Do | Go | | Go | Do |
| | | | | | Dun | | | | | | | | Dun | | |

# EXERCISE TEN    CD 5

This exercise is designed to 'wake up' your left and right hands, so that they can work independently of one another, as a further step away from playing pairs of strokes. Let one hand play one stroke all the time - say the right hand playing 'Go', and then let the other hand rotate between bass, tone and slap strokes. Keep playing right, left, right, left, right left.

Rpt.

| | | | | Ta | | | | | Ta |
|---|---|---|---|---|---|---|---|---|---|
| Go | | Go | Do | Go | Go | | Go | Do | Go |
| | Dun | | | | | Dun | | | |

Now swap over so your left hand stays in one place, and your right hand rotates.

Gun/Dun

Go/Do

Pa/Ta

# EXERCISE ELEVEN  CD 5

As a more complex variation of the previous exercise, you can let the 'stationary' hand alternate between two positions - eg tone & bass, whilst the other hand moves around from tone to bass to slap.

Eg: The right hand rotates; Gun, Pa, Go, Gun, Pa, Go, & rpt, whilst the left hand alternates; Dun, Do, Dun, Do, Dun, Do, & rpt.

The right hand pattern looks like this;

Rpt.

| | | Pa | | | | | | Pa | | | |
|---|---|---|---|---|---|---|---|---|---|---|---|
| | | | | Go | | | | | | Go | |
| Gun | | | | | | Gun | | | | | |

The left hand pattern looks like this;

| | | | | | | | | | | | |
|---|---|---|---|---|---|---|---|---|---|---|---|
| | | Do | | | | Do | | | | Do | |
| | Dun | | | | Dun | | | | Dun | | |

Together, they cycle like this ;

| | | Pa | | | | | Pa | | | |
|---|---|---|---|---|---|---|---|---|---|---|
| | | | Do | Go | | Do | | | Go | Do |
| Gun | Dun | | | | Dun | Gun | | Dun | | |

You can try swapping the 'roles' between the hands, to balance the exercise.

Gun/Dun

Go/Do

Pa/Ta

# EXERCISE TWELVE  CD 6

This easy rhythm is dominated by the left hand, which swings from Dun to Do and back all the time. Variations are then added.

### Variation 1

┌─ Rpt.

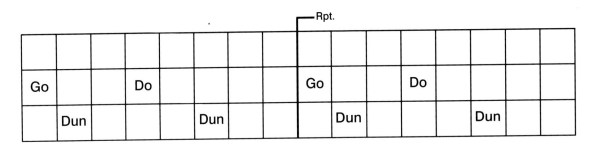

| | | | | | | | | | | | | | | | |
|---|---|---|---|---|---|---|---|---|---|---|---|---|---|---|---|
| Go | | | Do | | | | | Go | | | Do | | | | |
| | Dun | | | | Dun | | | | Dun | | | | Dun | | |

### Variation 2

┌─ Rpt.

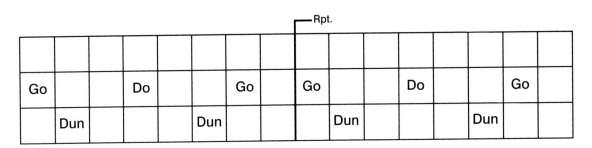

| | | | | | | | | | | | | | | | |
|---|---|---|---|---|---|---|---|---|---|---|---|---|---|---|---|
| Go | | | Do | | | Go | | Go | | | Do | | | Go | |
| | Dun | | | | Dun | | | | Dun | | | | Dun | | |

### Variation 3

┌─ Rpt.

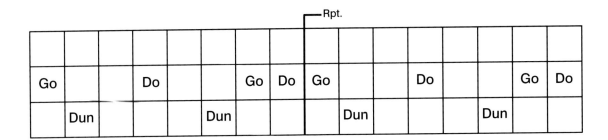

| | | | | | | | | | | | | | | | |
|---|---|---|---|---|---|---|---|---|---|---|---|---|---|---|---|
| Go | | | Do | | | Go | Do | Go | | | Do | | | Go | Do |
| | Dun | | | | Dun | | | | Dun | | | | Dun | | |

You can alternate the variations as much as you like, and try making up new ones.

NB The above exercises are a great introduction to using 'ghosting' in your playing, for the silent beats.

Gun/Dun

Go/Do

Pa/Ta

# EXERCISE THIRTEEN - TRIPLETS  CD 7

This is an excellent exercise, which many players use as a regular warm up. It has an easy, three beat pattern which can be very addictive. The trick is to keep your hands alternating right, left, right, left, right, left & rpt, and at the same time count in threes, 1, 2, 3, 1, 2, 3, 1, 2, 3, & rpt. This means that the count of 1 falls first on the right hand, then the left, then back to the right.

Start by playing edge tones, Go, Do, Go, Do, Go, Do etc

Now as you play, count out loud, 1, 2, 3, 1, 2, 3, 1, 2, 3, etc, without any gaps.

Now emphasise the '1' beat each time, by playing it a little louder. You will notice that the '1' beat swaps from one hand to the other.

Now move the '1' beat to the bass tone, so you are playing:

Bass, tone, tone, bass, tone, tone, bass, tone, tone, etc

|  |  |  |  |  |  | Rpt. |  |  |  |  |  |
|---|---|---|---|---|---|---|---|---|---|---|---|
|  | Do | Go |  | Go | Do |  | Do | Go |  | Go | Do |
| Gun |  |  | Dun |  |  | Gun |  |  | Dun |  |  |

Once you get familiar with the basic pattern, you can try playing variations, such as :

bass, tone, tone, bass, slap, slap

slap, tone, tone, slap, bass, bass

|  |  |  |  | Pa | Ta | Rpt. |  |  |  | Pa | Ta |
|---|---|---|---|---|---|---|---|---|---|---|---|
|  | Do | Go |  |  |  |  | Do | Go |  |  |  |
| Gun |  |  | Dun |  |  | Gun |  |  | Dun |  |  |

This variation misses the second beat of three of the triplets

|  |  |  |  |  |  |  |  |  |  |  |  |
|---|---|---|---|---|---|---|---|---|---|---|---|
|  |  | Go |  |  | Do |  |  | Go |  | Go | Do |
| Gun |  |  | Dun |  |  | Gun |  |  | Dun |  |  |

# EXERCISE FOURTEEN  CD 8

### EMPHASIS, AND THE 'SHAPE' OF A RHYTHM

Emphasis in a rhythm usually comes from hearing the bass and slap tones, as distinct from the edge tones. This will become clearer as you play more complex rhythms, and at greater speed. The 'shape' and 'feel' of the rhythm changes with the different strokes being emphasised, and with the number of strokes per repeat cycle.

We are now using genuine West African Rhythms!

| | | | | | | Rpt. | | | | | | |
|---|---|---|---|---|---|---|---|---|---|---|---|---|
| | | | | | | | | | | | | |
| Go | | | Do | Go | | | Go | | | Do | Go | |
| | | | | | Gun | | | | | | Gun | |

# EXERCISE FIFTEEN  CD 8

This exercise has a different 'feel' and 'shape' to the above - it's twice as long, with completely different emphasese.

| | | | | | | | | | Pa | | Ta | |
|---|---|---|---|---|---|---|---|---|---|---|---|---|
| Go | Do | | | | | Go | Do | | | | | |
| | | Gun | | Dun | | | | | | | | |

### SPEED, FLUENCY, AND TEMPO

The way that the exercises and rhythms are presented in this book does not indicate the speed of your playing - to play along a row of boxes may take five seconds, or it may take fifteen. As your experience grows, you will be able to play the exercises and rhythms with increasing speed and fluency, but you must be careful to keep your speed of playing under control - it's very tempting to increase in speed as you repeat a rhythm. Of course this is OK when you're on your own, and can allow you to discover the limits of your current ability, but if you are ever to play with other people in a group or band, it will be important to maintain the same speed. Musicians call this 'setting the tempo', and it allows everyone in the group to play together, without some rushing ahead, and some lagging behind. Remember - if you were the drummer in, say, a rock group, and your tempo was not absolutely rock steady, you would soon get thrown out of the group.

Gun/Dun

Go/Do

Pa/Ta

# EXERCISE SIXTEEN - TEMPO

 CD 9

The idea in this exercise is to be able to complete any single line in the same amount of time, even though the line have different numbers of strokes in them. Do not ghost in between the strokes - on the third line you only move your hands three times (quite slowly), whilst on the eighth line you move your hands eight times (quite quickly).

As you go through the exercise, you will realise that your hands must move twice as fast on line four, as on line two, to fit in twice as many strokes in the same amount of time. The same goes for line six, compared to line three. Line nine, (with sixteen strokes) is twice as fast as line eight, which has eight.

| Line 1 | Bass | | | | | | | | | | | | | | | | rpt |
|---|---|---|---|---|---|---|---|---|---|---|---|---|---|---|---|---|---|
| Line 2 | Bass | | | | | | | Tone | | | | | | | | | rpt |
| Line 3 | Bass | | | | | Tone | | | | | Tone | | | | | | rpt |
| Line 4 | Bass | | | Tone | | | Tone | | | Tone | | | | | | | rpt |
| Line 5 | Bass | | Tone | | Tone | | Tone | | Tone | | | | | | | | rpt |
| Line 6 | Bass | Tone | | Tone | | Tone | | Tone | | Tone | | | | | | | rpt |
| Line 7 | Bass | Tone | Tone | | Tone | | Tone | | Tone | | Tone | | | | | | rpt |
| Line 8 | Bass | Tone | Tone | Tone | | Tone | | Tone | | Tone | | Tone | | Tone | | | rpt |
| Line 9 | Bass | Tone | Tone | Tone | Tone | Tone | Tone | Tone | Tone | Tone | Tone | Tone | Tone | Tone | Tone | Tone | rpt |

## COMMON FORMS AND STRUCTURES

In West Africa, drumming is mainly taught by copying, and by one person singing or saying the rhythms to another, but Western students, particularly those who have studied classical music, often want to know what label to give to rhythm forms - eg is it a 4/4, a 6/8 a 3/4, a 12/8.

I have no formal/classical Western musical training, but I have come to understand that many parts fit with a background count of four, and others with a count of three. You can see the basis for this in exercise 16 above. Line three has a simple count of three, and line six can be counted 1,2,3,1,2,3 or as 1,&,2,&,3,&, both of which are easier than counting 1,2,3,4,5,6, when you have to keep repeating it.

Counting the easiest way that fits for line eight - 1,2,3,4,5,6,7,8 can be counted 1,&,2,&,3,&,4,&

This method of counting the easiest way can be applied to any repeating rhythm cycle - for instance a part with a count of sixteen (line 9) will often be counted as 1,e,&,a,2,e,&,a,3,e,&,a,4,e,&,a, which looks complex on paper, I admit, but is far easier to say out loud (or in your head) than the numbers - 1 to 16, or even 1,&,2,&,3,&,4,&,5,&,6,&,7,&,8,&.

The further you go into drumming and rhythm, the more fascinating this all becomes, and you will no doubt meet people who will talk about fantastic rhythm structures not discussed here. The furthest I go is to explain that some numbers - eg 12 - can be divided in different ways - ie 3x4 or 4x3 or 2x6, so in some cases the theorists are left discussing things after the drummers have played and gone home smiling. In African multi-part drumming you will often find different drums playing different length parts - one might cycle on threes, another on sixes, and another on twelves, or one might cycle on fours, another on eights, and another on sixteens, The further you go, the more you'll find.

It's another aspect of drum-addiction!

# Playing Djun Djun & Other Instruments

As mentioned before, the djembe is part of an ensemble of instruments which also includes bass drums (djun djun), bells, and hand percussion such as chekere (gourd based rattles) caxixi (basket rattles), rakatak (wood & gourd elbow shaped rattles) & kariyan ( a kind of metal guiro. Other drums such as wooden slit drums (kirin / kele) frame drums (siko) bowl drums, water drums and talking drums are also often played alongside the djembe. In this chapter we'll concentrate on the basic strokes for the djun djun, bells and hand percussion.

## DJUN DJUN  CD 10

Any combination of the three sizes of djun djun can be played together, and often only one drum is played (usually the djun djun or sangbani). The bass drums can be held horizontally on a stand, with the players beating the ends with wooden sticks or padded beaters. Often the bass drums have bells attached to them, and the player strikes the bell with one hand with a metal striker or drumstick, whilst playing the drum itself with the other hand. With the drum on its stand, (or on a chair or stool) it should be possible to comfortably strike the end of the drum with a big round ended stick or bass drum beater (try a surdo beater if you know any samba drummers). It's not necessary to hit it very hard, but as with most drums, you can use an open tone where you bounce the beater off the drum, or a closed tone, where you leave the beater on the drum to dampen the skin.

### ARRANGEMENT OF THE DJUN DJUN

The three djun djun are sometimes played by individual players, and sometimes all by one player. To achieve this they can be tied together in a stack so that all three drum heads can be reached by the same player. Only one bell would be played by this drummer, not three. Occasionally in the West, bass drums are played supported on a stand in a kind of 'African drum kit' arrangement. This can feel more accessible to a Western player than the vertical arrangement.

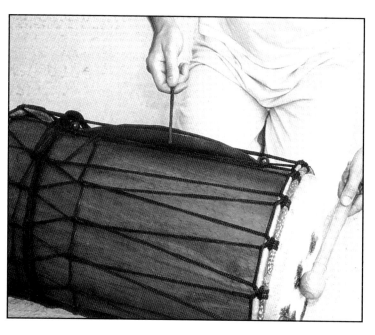

Playing djun djun

## BELLS  CD 10

There are lots of different shapes of iron bell to be found in West Africa. Very often a simple iron tube suffices as a bell, when it's tied to the side of a drum. An advance on this is the pod shaped apitua (or banana gong) which is formed rather like a large, opened pea pod (with the peas removed). It can be anything from four inches to ten inches long, is either hand held or tied to the djun djun, and is played with an iron striker similar to a large nail. If it's played in the hand, the tone can be changed by gripping with the fingers, and can be open or closed according to the type of strike, as above.

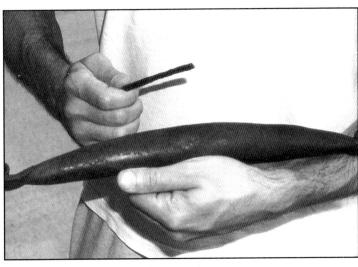

Playing apitua

Another kind of bell is the iron agogo (African agogo), which is a double bell with a small and large part which sound approximately an octave apart. This is

made of thinner iron than the apitua, and can be played with a lighter stick, such as an average wooden drum stick. Patterns can be played between the upper and lower bell, and the larger bell can be 'wowed' against your body like the gourd of a berimbau. Both upper and lower tones can be played open or closed, as above, according to the way you strike them.

## CHEKERE  CD 10

The chekere ( or chekere cabassa, or yabara) is made by tying a net of seeds or beads around the empty, hollow body of a dry gourd. The net is quite loose so the beads can rattle against the gourd.

The most popular type of gourd is one which grows with a handle shaped protruberance, and this handle is held in one hand to shake the chekere. Another type is made with the handle missing - this is often much larger and can be hung around the player's neck and played with both hands to give a rhythm from either the net of beads or from the body of the gourd itself.

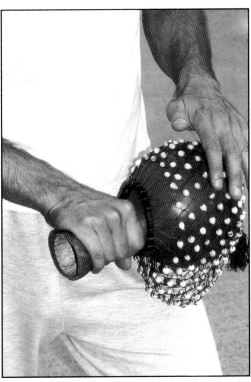

Playing chekere

Playing agogo

## CAXIXI  CD 10

Caxixi are woven rattles which can be made from any basket type materials such as grass or cane, and come in 'single' and 'double' forms. Most commonly they are eight to twelve inches high, and look a bit like bottles made of woven grass. Inside are seeds or beads which rattle against the body when it is shaken, and often there is a piece of gourd woven into the body (usually the 'base' of the 'bottle') which gives a different sound when the beads hit it. The two clearly different sounds of the caxixi can be made by simply turning it as you shake it so that the beads inside will hit either the grass weave, or the gourd base.

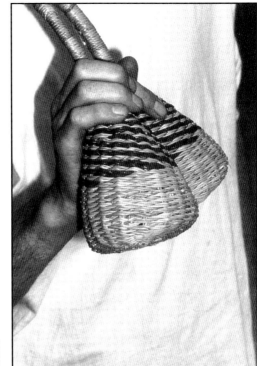

Playing caxixi

Playing caxixi

## RAKATAK  CD 10

Rakatak are rattles made from wooden elbows (angled sticks) with discs of gourd threaded onto one part of the elbow. The other part of the elbow is held in the hand for shaking. The rakatak (also known as wasamba and wooden sistrums) is an ancient instrument said to date back to the Middle Ages, and is often used during ceremonies such as circumcision to ward off spirits, and to warn villagers of the whereabouts of persons they should not approach. In this it is similar to the Aboriginal bull-roarer in Australia.

Playing rakatak

Usually played in pairs, the rakatak are shaken up and down so that the discs rattle loudly against each other. It is said that some advanced players can make the two sets of gourd discs rub against each other as they move, to give a variety of different sounds and rhythms.

# Part Three

Group Drumming

# Easy Multi-part Rhythms For Groups

## MULTI-PART PLAYING

If you've ever watched a drumming group you will of course know that different members of the group play different parts. Putting two or more rhythm parts together at the same time can be quite difficult at first - the part that you are not playing tends to interfere with the part that you are playing, but it gets easier with practice. I think the trick is to get very familiar with your own part, then let part of your mind concentrate on getting it right, whilst the other part of your mind listens to the group as a whole, to check things like speed, and volume. Each player needs to be playing at approximately the same volume - if you can't hear all the other parts, someone is playing too loud, and it might be you !

Try the rhythms on the following pages - you don't have to use all the parts at once, and you can make up your own parts as much as you like, but remember - most multi-part rhythms have developed over many years by players experimenting, and settling on parts which sound good together. The rhythms which follow in the rest of the book were all taught to me by experienced drummers in various styles. They are credited in the acknowledgments page, on page 56, and in appendix 1.

## SOME NOTES ON DRUMMER HEALTH AND DRUM- ADDICTION

Generally it's recognised that drumming - particularly in groups - is good for you. You are being rhythmically and musically creative in your own life, you are sharing a group experience and interacting with other people, and you are participating in a physical exercise which engages some important, and often under-used muscle groups. However, it's important to be aware that drumming can be quite addictive, and as you get deeper into it, you will need to look after yourself in the following ways.

**HAND CARE** - Take great care of your hands. Take the time to learn the correct way to hit each stroke, and try not to play hard. It's very tempting to throw your hands at the drum to get more volume in a group situation, but bruises the next day can be very off-putting. As you gain experience, you will be able to play louder, without losing control of your hand positions.

Look after your hands

**EAR CARE** - I saw an article on the internet once about the decibel levels produced by groups of Samba drummers. It suggested that when a group of ten to twenty drummers play together - particularly when they play or rehearse indoors - the decibel levels produced would only be considered safe for about five minutes exposure. Of course, many groups practice for a couple of hours, and the same is true of most African drum/djembe groups. This noise level can leave your ears ringing for several hours afterwards - usually only a minor inconvenience, but prolonged exposure can cause a condition called Tinnitus, which is described as permanent, incurable ringing in the ears. The only treatment for this - as at August 1999 - is distraction, i.e. you have to think about something else. Tinnitus is a serious

condition which could affect your ability to hear for the rest of your life, but thankfully, you can avoid the risk by getting hold of little earplugs from your local chemist (pharmacist) and wearing them if you think the group you are in is getting too big or too loud, or both. Don't let anybody call you sissy - it's not worth the risk.

**POSTURE** - As a teacher and group leader for several years I've come to realise that drumming can make you ache in places where you didn't even know you had places. This happens to many people, and I realised over the years that the places where drummers get their aches and pains correspond closely to how they are postured when they play. For many people, the drumming posture is similar the writing posture, and it has developed over many years since they were children in primary school. There are many techniques for developing better posture, which are beyond the scope of this book, but it must be worth saying that recognising your own points of tension is always the first step towards improvement. Really - hunching your shoulders, frowning, leaning to one side, even lounging in your chair, none of these postures will help you play with fluidity. If you unlock the energy which is being used to keep these postures, that extra energy will be useful for playing your drum more expressively.

# RHYTHM ONE - A first exercise in multi-part  CD 11

Try this first exercise with your group. The four parts are very simple on their own - get thoroughly familiar with each one before you start layering them on top of each other. Remember, you all have to play at the same speed, but part four starts after the other three parts have started, because the first stroke is a 'ghost' stroke.

**Part one**

Rpt.

| | | | | | | | | | | | | | | | |
|---|---|---|---|---|---|---|---|---|---|---|---|---|---|---|---|
| Go | | Go | | Go | Do | Go | | Go | | Go | | Go | Do | Go | |
| | | | | | | | | | | | | | | | |

**Part two**

Rpt.

| | | | | | | | | | | | | | | | |
|---|---|---|---|---|---|---|---|---|---|---|---|---|---|---|---|
| Pa | Ta | | | Pa | Ta | Pa | | Pa | Ta | | | Pa | Ta | Pa | |
| | | | | | | | | | | | | | | | |
| | | | | | | | | | | | | | | | |

**Part three**

Rpt.

| | | | | | | | | | | | | | | | |
|---|---|---|---|---|---|---|---|---|---|---|---|---|---|---|---|
| | | | | | | | | | | | | | | | |
| Gun | | Gun | | Gun | | Gun | Dun | Gun | | Gun | | Gun | | Gun | Dun |

**Part four**

Rpt.

| | | | | | | | | | | | | | | | |
|---|---|---|---|---|---|---|---|---|---|---|---|---|---|---|---|
| | Do | | Do | | Do | Go | Do | | Do | | Do | | Do | Go | Do |
| | | | | | | | | | | | | | | | |

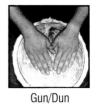

Gun/Dun

Go/Do

Pa/Ta

# RHYTHM TWO - 'Aconcon'   CD 12

This simple version of Aconcon uses two identical parts, but the second part follows after the first part, and constantly echoes it.

**Part one** - good for working your left hand

Rpt.

| | | | | | Pa | | | | | | | | Pa | | |
|---|---|---|---|---|---|---|---|---|---|---|---|---|---|---|---|
| Do | | Do | | Do | | Do | | Do | | Do | | Do | | Do | |
| | Gun | | | | | | | Gun | | | | | | | |

**Part two** - the 'do' in brackets is only played when the cycle repeats - not when you first start.

Rpt.

| | | | | | | | Pa | | | | | | | | Pa |
|---|---|---|---|---|---|---|---|---|---|---|---|---|---|---|---|
| (Do) | | Do | | Do | | Do | | Do | | Do | | Do | | | |
| | | | Gun | | | | | | | Gun | | | | | |

Gun/Dun

Go/Do

Pa/Ta

# RHYTHM THREE - 'Jabba Jabba Djembe'  CD 13

This simple multi-part is great fun, and uses just bass and tone strokes most of the time.

## Part one

| | | | | | | | Rpt. | | | | | | | | |
|---|---|---|---|---|---|---|---|---|---|---|---|---|---|---|---|
| Go | Do | Go | Do | | | | | Go | Do | Go | Do | | | | |
| | | | Gun | | Gun | | | | | | | Gun | | Gun | |

## Part two

| | | | | | | | | | | | | | | | Rpt. |
|---|---|---|---|---|---|---|---|---|---|---|---|---|---|---|---|
| | | | | | | | | | | | | Pa | | | |
| | | | | Go | Do | Go | Do | | | | | | | | |
| Gun | | Gun | | | | | | Gun | | Gun | | | | | |

## Part three - has a very different timing and feel

| | | | | | | | | | | | | | | | Rpt. |
|---|---|---|---|---|---|---|---|---|---|---|---|---|---|---|---|
| | | | | | | | | | | | | Pa | | | |
| | | | | | | | | Go | Do | Go | Do | | | | |
| Gun | | | Gun | | | | | | | | | | | | |

After a few moments you will hear the phrase GoDoGoDo rotating around the three parts, followed by the slap from parts two and three.

Gun/Dun

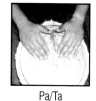
Go/Do

Pa/Ta

# RHYTHM FOUR - 'Afro-Cuban'  CD 14

This is a simple two part version of the Afro Cuban rhythm in the next chapter

## Part one - ghosting version

Rpt.

| | | | | | | | | | | | | | | | |
|---|---|---|---|---|---|---|---|---|---|---|---|---|---|---|---|
| Go | | | | | Do | | | Go | | | | | Do | | |
| | | Gun | | | | Gun | | | | Gun | | | | Gun | |

## Part one - hand to hand version

Rpt.

| | | | | | | | | | | | | | | | |
|---|---|---|---|---|---|---|---|---|---|---|---|---|---|---|---|
| Go | | | | | Go | | | Go | | | | | Go | | |
| | | Dun | | | | Dun | | | | Dun | | | | Dun | |

## Part two - the PA stroke in brackets is only played when the cycle repeats, not at the beginning.

Rpt.

| | | | | | | | | | | | | | | | |
|---|---|---|---|---|---|---|---|---|---|---|---|---|---|---|---|
| (Pa) | | | | | | | | Pa | | | | | | | |
| | | Go | Do | | | Go | Do | | | Go | Do | | | Go | Do |
| | | | | | | | | | | | | | | | |

Gun/Dun

Go/Do

Pa/Ta

# RHYTHM FIVE - 'Lamin'   CD 15

This is created by simply combining exercises 14 & 15 from chapter 5, which you will be familiar with. The full seven part rhythm is presented in chapter eight, as 'Rhythm for a Gambian Song'.

**Part one**

Rpt.

| | | | | | | | | | | | | | | | |
|---|---|---|---|---|---|---|---|---|---|---|---|---|---|---|---|
| | | | | | | | | | | | | | | | |
| Go | | | Do | Go | | | | Go | | | Do | Go | | | |
| | | | | | Gun | | | | | | | | | Gun | |

**Part two**

Start    Rpt.

| | | | | | | | | | | | | | | | |
|---|---|---|---|---|---|---|---|---|---|---|---|---|---|---|---|
| | | | | | | | Pa | | | Ta | | | | | |
| | | | | | Go | Do | | | | | | | Go | Do | |
| Gun | | | Dun | | | | | | | | | | | | |

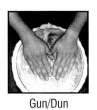

Gun/Dun

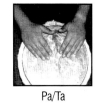

Go/Do

Pa/Ta

# RHYTHM SIX - 'Shaman'   CD 16

### Djembe one
The three offbeat TA strokes can be tricky unless your left hand is awake!

| | | | | | | | | | | | | | | | |
|---|---|---|---|---|---|---|---|---|---|---|---|---|---|---|---|
| Pa | | Pa | | | | Ta | | Ta | | Ta | | | | | |
| | | | | | | | | | | | | | | | |
| | | | Gun | | | | | | | | | Gun | | | |

### Djembe two
Shaman rhythm has four 'bars' in part two - the first three are the same, but be ready for a change in bar four.

| | | | | | | | | | | | | | | | |
|---|---|---|---|---|---|---|---|---|---|---|---|---|---|---|---|
| | | Pa | Ta | | | Pa | Ta | | | Pa | Ta | | | Pa | Ta |
| | | | | | | | | | | | | | | | |
| Gun | | | | | | | | Gun | | | | | | | |

| | | | | | | | | | | | | | | | |
|---|---|---|---|---|---|---|---|---|---|---|---|---|---|---|---|
| | | Pa | Ta | | | Pa | Ta | | | | | | | | |
| | | | | | | | | | | | | | | | |
| Gun | | | | | | | | Gun | | Gun | | Gun | | Gun | |

### Bass drum part - use one drum or alternate between two

| | | | | | | | | | | | | | | | |
|---|---|---|---|---|---|---|---|---|---|---|---|---|---|---|---|
| X | | | | X | | | | X | | | | X | | | |

### Bell part - count 1,2,3,4, hitting the bell on 3 and 4.

| | | | | | | | | | | | | | | | |
|---|---|---|---|---|---|---|---|---|---|---|---|---|---|---|---|
| | | X | X | | | X | X | | | X | X | | | X | X |

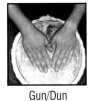
Gun/Dun

Go/Do

Pa/Ta

# RHYTHM SEVEN - 'Soli'  CD 17

This again is a simple version of Soli, which is presented in full in the next chapter.

**Djembe one** is a very simple part, with no complications.

|  |  |  |  |  |  | Rpt. |  |  |  |  |  |
|---|---|---|---|---|---|---|---|---|---|---|---|
| Pa |  |  | Ta |  |  | Pa |  |  | Ta |  |  |
|  |  | Go |  |  |  |  |  | Go |  |  |  |
|  |  |  |  |  |  |  |  |  |  |  |  |

**Djembe two** starts with the left hand TA, except on starting, when a PA puts it into the right place. When played properly, djembes one and two are playing TA and PA at the same time.

|  |  |  |  |  |  | Rpt. |  |  |  |  |  |
|---|---|---|---|---|---|---|---|---|---|---|---|
| (Pa) |  |  | Ta |  |  | Pa |  |  | Ta |  |  |
|  |  |  |  | Go | Do |  |  |  |  | Go | Do |
|  |  |  |  |  |  |  |  |  |  |  |  |

A bell and/or bass drum can accompany, striking two and three, out of every count of three - i.e. count 1,2,3,1,2,3,1,2,3 etc in your head, and strike each count of  2 and 3

|  | X | X |  | X | X |  | X | X |  | X | X |
|---|---|---|---|---|---|---|---|---|---|---|---|

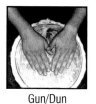

Gun/Dun

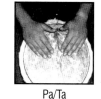

Go/Do

Pa/Ta

# RHYTHM EIGHT - 'Threes against fours'  CD 18

This may be the most challenging of all these simple rhythms, because the element of poly-rhythm is strongest. Strictly speaking, poly-rhythm is more than just playing multiple parts at the same time - the parts should really have a different rhythmic basis, such that they weave together in a more complex way. This means that the players will be counting in different ways.

In this rhythm, part one is counted in fours - i.e. 1 & 2 & 3 & 4 & 1 & 2 & 3 & 4 &, but part two is counted in threes - i.e. 1 2 3 1 2 3 1 2 3 1 2 3 . When you put these two parts together, the count of '1' falls at different times, and they only come together every so often. Mathematically, it sounds very simple, and the individual parts are very simple as well, but putting them together is - well, try it for yourself. The ghost strokes and longer rhythm cycle of part one make it seem 'slower', whilst the short cycle and lack of ghost strokes in part two make it seem faster, but each player's hands should be moving at the same speed.

Also note that because part two is counted in threes, and three is an odd number, the hands alternate as you go along - i.e., the bass tone is played first with the right hand, then with the left hand. This was exercise 13, from chapter 5.

**Djembe one** - (this can be played on Go/Do if you prefer)

*Rpt. begins at column 8.*

| Pa |  | Pa | Ta |  | Ta | Pa |  | Pa |  | Pa | Ta |  | Ta | Pa |  |
|----|----|----|----|----|----|----|----|----|----|----|----|----|----|----|----|
|  |  |  |  |  |  |  |  |  |  |  |  |  |  |  |  |
|  |  |  |  |  |  |  |  |  |  |  |  |  |  |  |  |

**Djembe two**

*Rpt. begins at column 8.*

|  |  |  |  |  |  |  |  |  |  |  |  |  |  |  |  |
|----|----|----|----|----|----|----|----|----|----|----|----|----|----|----|----|
|  | Do | Go |  | Go | Do |  |  | Do | Go |  | Go | Do |  | Do | Go |
| Gun |  |  | Dun |  |  | Gun |  |  | Dun |  |  | Gun |  |  | Gun |

**Bell**

*Rpt. begins at column 8.*

|  |  |  |  |  |  |  |  |  |  |  |  |  |  |  |  |
|----|----|----|----|----|----|----|----|----|----|----|----|----|----|----|----|
| X |  |  |  | X | X |  | X | X |  |  |  | X | X |  | X |
|  |  |  |  |  |  |  |  |  |  |  |  |  |  |  |  |

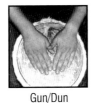
Gun/Dun

Go/Do

Pa/Ta

# TWO EXERCISES IN POLY-RHYTHM FOR ONE PERSON

Here are two examples of how one person can play two different rhythms at the same time - one on each hand! In both cases the left and right hands will stay in the same position on the drum for the sake of simplicity. The first exercise contains a beat of three played against a beat of two, and the second exercise contains a simple 4/4 beat played against a 3/2 clave beat.

**Exercise one - 'Three against Two'**  CD 19

For every two strokes on the left hand there are three played on the right hand. If you find it tricky, listen carefully to the cd and use the phrase - both, right left right.

Rpt.

| | | | | | | | | | | | |
|---|---|---|---|---|---|---|---|---|---|---|---|
| Go | | Go | | Go | | Go | | Go | | Go | |
| Dun | | | Dun | | | Dun | | | Dun | | |

**Exercise two - '4/4 against 3/2 clave'**  CD 19

This exercise is designed to illustrate how a fundamental African beat - the 3/2 clave fits against a simple 4/4 beat. Please note that the 3/2 clave is in itself a 'complex' rhythm which arises from two separate beats, which many Western players distort when they first try to play it. Make sure you play the first three beats with perfectly equal spacing - listen to the cd if you are not sure.

Rpt.

| | | | | | | | | | | | | | | | |
|---|---|---|---|---|---|---|---|---|---|---|---|---|---|---|---|
| Go | | | Go | | | Go | | | | Go | | Go | | | |
| Dun | | | | Dun | | | | Dun | | | | Dun | | | |

**Variations in the 3/2 clave beat**  CD 19

You will come across many variations of the 3/2 clave - some musics even use an upside down form called 2/3 clave. Two simple variations which you can create now simply involve moving the last 'Go' either one box or two boxes forward.

**Variation one**

| | | | | | | | | | | | | | | | |
|---|---|---|---|---|---|---|---|---|---|---|---|---|---|---|---|
| Go | | | Go | | | Go | | | | Go | | | Go | | |

**Variation two -** This variation is used in the Gahu rhythm in chapter 8

| | | | | | | | | | | | | | | | |
|---|---|---|---|---|---|---|---|---|---|---|---|---|---|---|---|
| Go | | | Go | | | Go | | | | Go | | | | Go | |

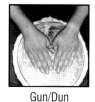

Gun/Dun

Go/Do

Pa/Ta

# Twelve West African Rhythms

The following rhythms are offered as an introduction to multi-part drumming with a genuine West African feel. I make no apology for the fact that some of them, if not all, are presented in a manner which simplifies them for consumption by beginners and for easier learning. I do not claim authorship of the original rhythms, and I have changed some of them from how they were originally taught to me, but I present here the versions which we currently play on a weekly basis in classes and groups in Leeds. Every drummer, including myself, learns their rhythms from someone else, through a variety of media, including personal teaching. For this reason, I acknowledge the sources of these rhythms as being the teachers who have brought them to me and many others. Who taught these teachers, I don't know.

**Rhythm 1 - 'Kpanlogo' -** This is a very simple approximation of a Ghanaian Kpanlogo, taught to me by Roger Wolfe in Ilkley in about 1995. Kpanlogo is played in Ghana on a Kpanlogo set, not on djembes, but the value of this rhythm is in it's accessibility.

**Rhythm 2 - 'Gahu' -** another extremely simplified approximation of a Ghanaian dance. The Gahu pokes fun at the influence of the West on Africans who travel there. The arrangement presented here is my own modification of one taught by Jobina Pinkenburg to Pierre La Blanche, whose group I attended on the Cape coast of South Africa in 1998. I believe I've taken it back a little closer to the Ghanaian original, by re-inserting a Gahu bell part, and modifying parts one and two.

**Rhythm 3 - 'Afro-Cuban'-** A beautifully laid back rhythm from the Caribbean, which I have adapted from Jim Griener's presentation on the Latin Percussion tuition video 'Community Drumming'.

**Rhythm 4 - 'Kuku' -** This is not the only rhythm I've heard being called Kuku, but it is the one I call Kuku. Arrangement by Jobina Pinkenburg, and taught by Pierre

La Blanche in South Africa, 1998 - a much loved rhythm in Yorkshire!

**Rhythm 5 - Kassagbe -** a beautifully simple Guinean rhythm, laid out as taught by American teacher Paulo Mattioli in his excellent tuition video series 'Hands on Drumming'.

**Rhythm 6 - A Gambian Song -** as taught and played by Leeds based Gambian drummer Lamin Jassey, this is one of two songs presented in full on his tuition cassette 'Lamin Jassey- djembe drum tuition'.

**Rhythm 7 - 'Fanti' -** third one from the South African group, Fanti is a complex, uplifting rhythm which we often use as an interlude in Kuku. Note that the djun djun follows the bell, which plays the count of one, and enjoy the cascading effect of TA - DO GO DO in part two.

**Rhythm 8 : Macrou, Rhythm 9 : Soli, Rhythm 10 : Kassa, Rhythm 11 : Yankadi -** Guinean rhythms from the 'Hands on Drumming' videos, arranged by Paulo Mattioli. From Soli onwards we leave behind the count of four, and enter the more complex world of triplets sixes, and twelves. These rhythms all have the full complement of bass drum & bell parts, which tend to look daunting, but are easy when you hear them. Generally the djundjun and kenkeni will follow their bells quite closely, and one player should manage them with just a bit of practice, whilst the sangbani has a tendency for crossing its own bell part. If you get stuck, get separate people for the sangbani/bell parts.

**Rhythm 12 - Carabali -** an uplifting Afro-Cuban carnival rhythm named after, and probably rooted in, the Nigerian region of Calabar. Very easy djembe and bell parts are crossed wildly by the djundjun, which veers from on-beat to off-beat and back in a very powerful way. Sourced from Thomas Christen's 'MU SUM BA' World Drumming Workshop cassette 1995.

The basic shape is cut with adze and chisel

# KPANLOGO (count in fours)   ◎ CD 20

## DJEMBE 1

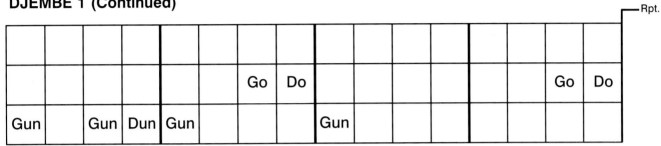

| | | | | | | | | | | | | | | | |
|---|---|---|---|---|---|---|---|---|---|---|---|---|---|---|---|
| | | | | | | | | | | | | | | | |
| | | | | | Go | Do | | | | | | | | Go | Do |
| Gun | | | | | | | | Gun | | | | | | | |

## DJEMBE 1 (Continued)

Rpt.

| | | | | | | | | | | | | | | | |
|---|---|---|---|---|---|---|---|---|---|---|---|---|---|---|---|
| | | | | | | | | | | | | | | | |
| | | | | | Go | Do | | | | | | | | Go | Do |
| Gun | | Gun | Dun | Gun | | | | Gun | | | | | | | |

## DJEMBE 2

Rpt.

| | | | | | | | | | | | | | | | |
|---|---|---|---|---|---|---|---|---|---|---|---|---|---|---|---|
| | | | | | | | | | | | | | | | |
| Go | | Go | | | | | | Go | Do | Go | Do | | | | |
| | | | | Gun | | | | | | | | Gun | | | |

## DJUNDJUN - 4/4 beat

| | | | | | | | | | | | | | | | |
|---|---|---|---|---|---|---|---|---|---|---|---|---|---|---|---|
| X | | | | X | | | | X | | | | X | | | |

## BELL - 3/2 clave

| | | | | | | | | | | | | | | | |
|---|---|---|---|---|---|---|---|---|---|---|---|---|---|---|---|
| X | | | X | | | X | | | | X | | X | | | |

## DJEMBE 3

Rpt.

| | | | | | | | | | | | | | | | |
|---|---|---|---|---|---|---|---|---|---|---|---|---|---|---|---|
| | | Pa | Ta | | | Pa | Ta | | | Pa | Ta | | | Pa | Ta |
| | | | | | | | | | | | | | | | |
| Gun | | | | Gun | | | | Gun | | | | Gun | | | |

Smoothing rough edges

# GAHU (count in fours)   CD 21

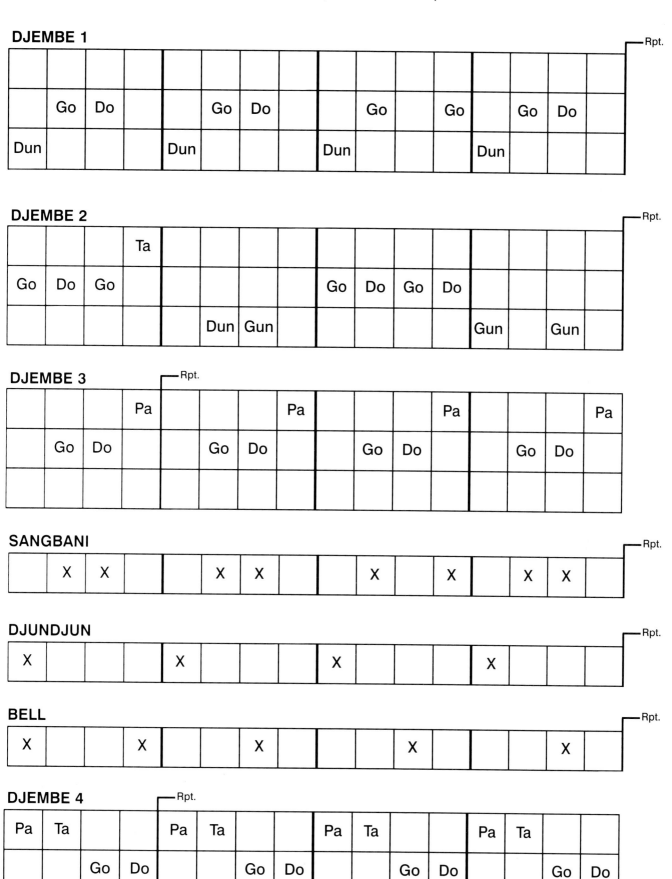

Alternatively play 4 slaps, 4 tones
or 3 slaps, 3 tones.

Tuning rings are custom made for each drum

# AFRO-CUBAN (count in fours)  CD 22

**DJEMBE 1**

| | | | | | | | | | | | | | | | |
|---|---|---|---|---|---|---|---|---|---|---|---|---|---|---|---|
| | | | Go | | | Go | | | | | Go | | | Go | |
| Dun | | | | Dun | | | | Dun | | | | Dun | | | |

**DJEMBE 1 (Continued)**  — Rpt.

| | | | | | | | | | Ta | Pa | | | | | |
|---|---|---|---|---|---|---|---|---|---|---|---|---|---|---|---|
| | | | Go | | | Go | | | | | Go | | | Go | |
| Dun | | | | Dun | | | | | | | | Dun | | | |

**DJEMBE 2**  — Rpt.

| | | | | | | | | | | | | | | Pa | |
|---|---|---|---|---|---|---|---|---|---|---|---|---|---|---|---|
| Go | Do | | | Go | Do | | | Go | Do | | Do | Go | Do | | |
| | | | | | | | | | | | | | | | |

**BELL** - 3/2 clave variation one (see page 56)

| | | | | | | | | | | | | | | | |
|---|---|---|---|---|---|---|---|---|---|---|---|---|---|---|---|
| X | | | X | | | X | | | | X | | | X | | |

**DJUNDJUN** - 4/4 beat

| | | | | | | | | | | | | | | | |
|---|---|---|---|---|---|---|---|---|---|---|---|---|---|---|---|
| X | | | X | | | X | | | X | | | | | | |

Parts and tools are gathered together

# KUKU (count in fours)   CD 23

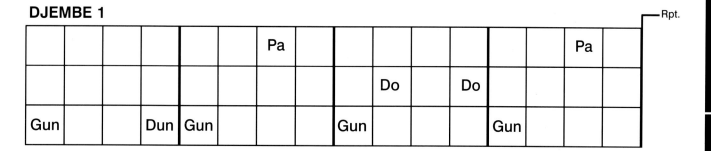

**DJEMBE 1**

| | | | | | | | | | | | | | | | | Rpt. |
|---|---|---|---|---|---|---|---|---|---|---|---|---|---|---|---|---|
| | | | | | Pa | | | | | | | | | Pa | | |
| | | | | | | | | | Do | | Do | | | | | |
| Gun | | | Dun | Gun | | | | Gun | | | | Gun | | | | |

**DJEMBE 2**

| | | | | | | | Rpt. | | | | | | | | |
|---|---|---|---|---|---|---|---|---|---|---|---|---|---|---|---|
| | | | | | Pa | | | | | | | | | Pa | |
| | | Go | Do | | | | | | | Go | Do | | | | |
| Gun | Dun | | | Gun | | | | Gun | Dun | | | Gun | | | |

**DJEMBE 3**

| | | | | | | | Rpt. | | | | | | | | |
|---|---|---|---|---|---|---|---|---|---|---|---|---|---|---|---|
| | | | | | | | | | | | | | | | |
| Go | Do | | Do | Go | Do | Go | | Go | Do | | Do | Go | Do | Go | |

**DJUNDJUN**

| | | | | | | | | | | | | | | | | Rpt. |
|---|---|---|---|---|---|---|---|---|---|---|---|---|---|---|---|---|
| X | | | X | X | | | | X | | | | X | | | | |

**BELL**

| | | | | | | Rpt. | | | | | | | | |
|---|---|---|---|---|---|---|---|---|---|---|---|---|---|---|
| | X | | X | | | X | | | X | | X | | | X | |

The rings are wrapped in cloth and rope loops are tied on

# KASSAGBE (count in fours)

 CD 24

**DJEMBE 1**  — Rpt.

| | | Pa | | | Pa | | | Pa | | | Pa | |
|---|---|---|---|---|---|---|---|---|---|---|---|---|
| | | | Do | | Do | | | | | | | |
| Gun | Dun | | | | | | Gun | Dun | | Gun | Dun | |

**DJEMBE 2**  — Rpt.

| | | | | | Pa | | | | | | Pa | |
|---|---|---|---|---|---|---|---|---|---|---|---|---|
| Go | Do | Go | Do | | | Go | Do | Go | Do | | | |
| | | | | | | | | | | | | |

**BELL**  — Rpt.

| X | | X | X | | X | | X | X | | X | X | | X | | X |
|---|---|---|---|---|---|---|---|---|---|---|---|---|---|---|---|

**KENKENI**

| | | | | | | | | | | | | | X | | X | |
|---|---|---|---|---|---|---|---|---|---|---|---|---|---|---|---|---|

**DJUNDJUN**

| X | X | | X | | X | X | | | | | | | | | |
|---|---|---|---|---|---|---|---|---|---|---|---|---|---|---|---|---|

The playing edge is checked and smoothed

# RHYTHM FOR A GAMBIAN SONG

(count in fours)

CD 25

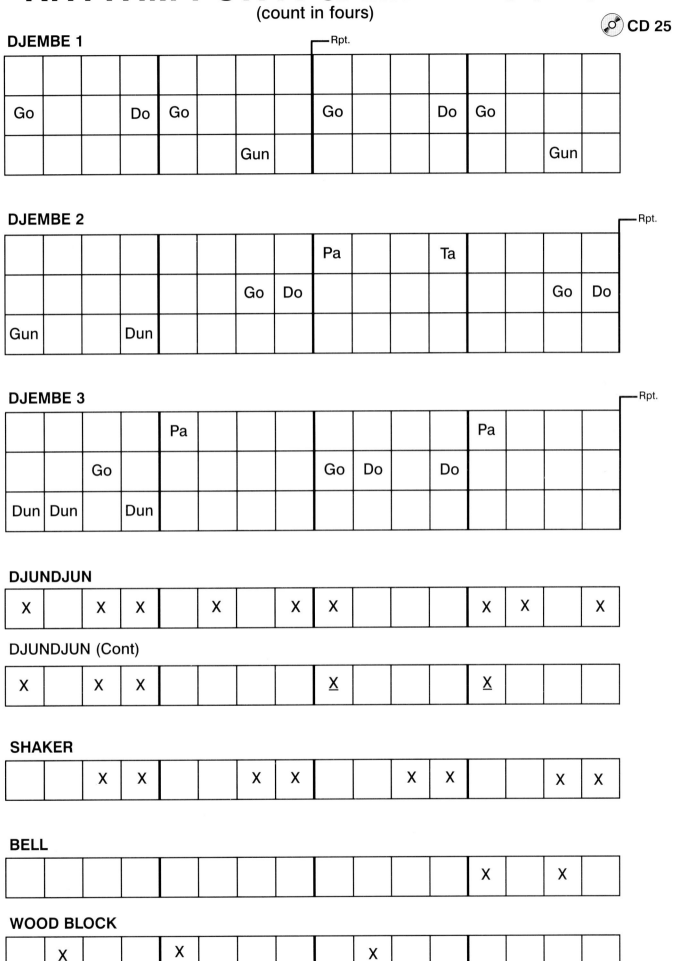

**DJEMBE 1**

**DJEMBE 2**

**DJEMBE 3**

**DJUNDJUN**

**DJUNDJUN (Cont)**

**SHAKER**

**BELL**

**WOOD BLOCK**

The goat skin is soaked in water

# FANTI (count in fours)    CD 26

**DJEMBE 1**   — Rpt.

| | | | | | Pa | | | | | | | | | | |
|---|---|---|---|---|---|---|---|---|---|---|---|---|---|---|---|
| | | | | | | | | | | | | | Do | Go | Do |
| Gun | | | | Dun | Gun | | | | Gun | | | Dun | Gun | | |

**DJEMBE 2**   — Rpt.

| | | Pa | | | | | | | | | Ta | | | | |
|---|---|---|---|---|---|---|---|---|---|---|---|---|---|---|---|
| | | Do | Go | Do | Go | | | | | | | | Do | Go | Do |
| Gun | Dun | | | | | | | Gun | Dun | | | | | | |

**DJEMBE 3**   — Rpt.

| | | | Ta | | | Pa | | | | | Ta | | | Pa | |
|---|---|---|---|---|---|---|---|---|---|---|---|---|---|---|---|
| Go | Do | | | Go | Do | | | Go | Do | | | Go | Do | | |
| | | | | | | | | | | | | | | | |

**DJUNDJUN** (follows Bell)   — Rpt.

| | | X | | | | X | | | X | X | | | | X | |
|---|---|---|---|---|---|---|---|---|---|---|---|---|---|---|---|

**BELL** (on the on-beat)   — Rpt.

| X | X | | | X | X | | | X | | | | X | X | | |
|---|---|---|---|---|---|---|---|---|---|---|---|---|---|---|---|

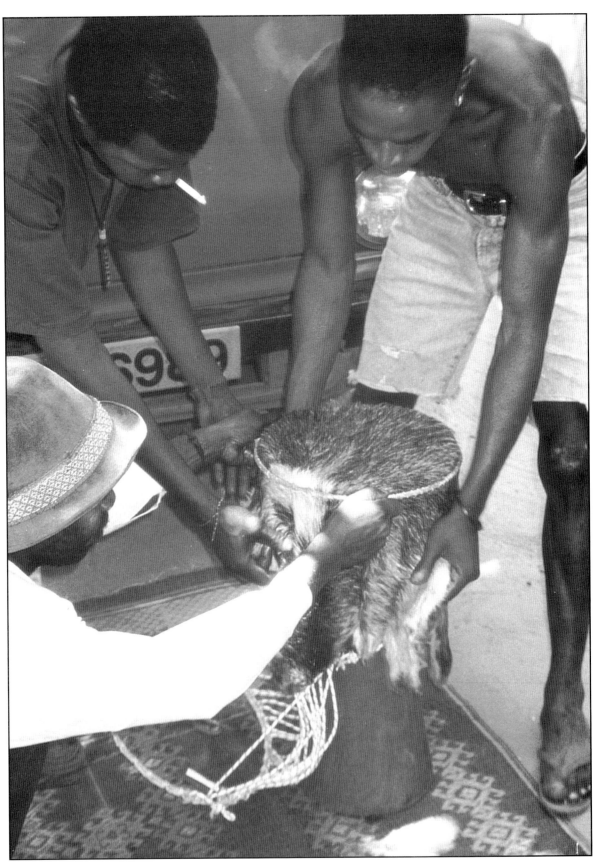

The wet skin is held on a drum by the rings

# MACROU (count in fours)  CD 27

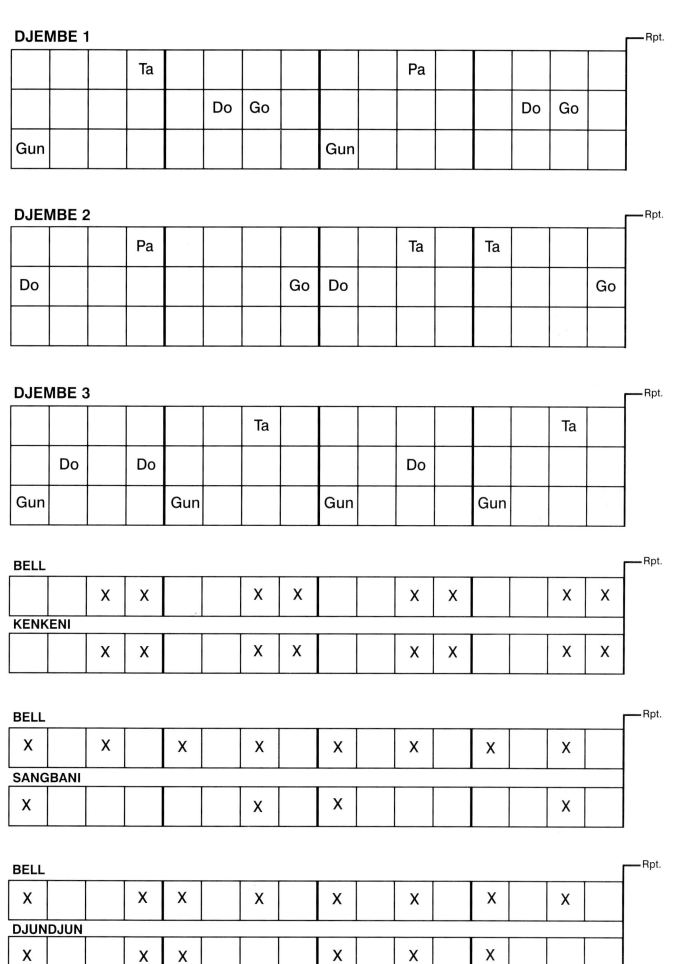

Tuning rope is woven through the loops whilst the skin is wet

# SOLI (6/8 - count in sixes)

CD 28

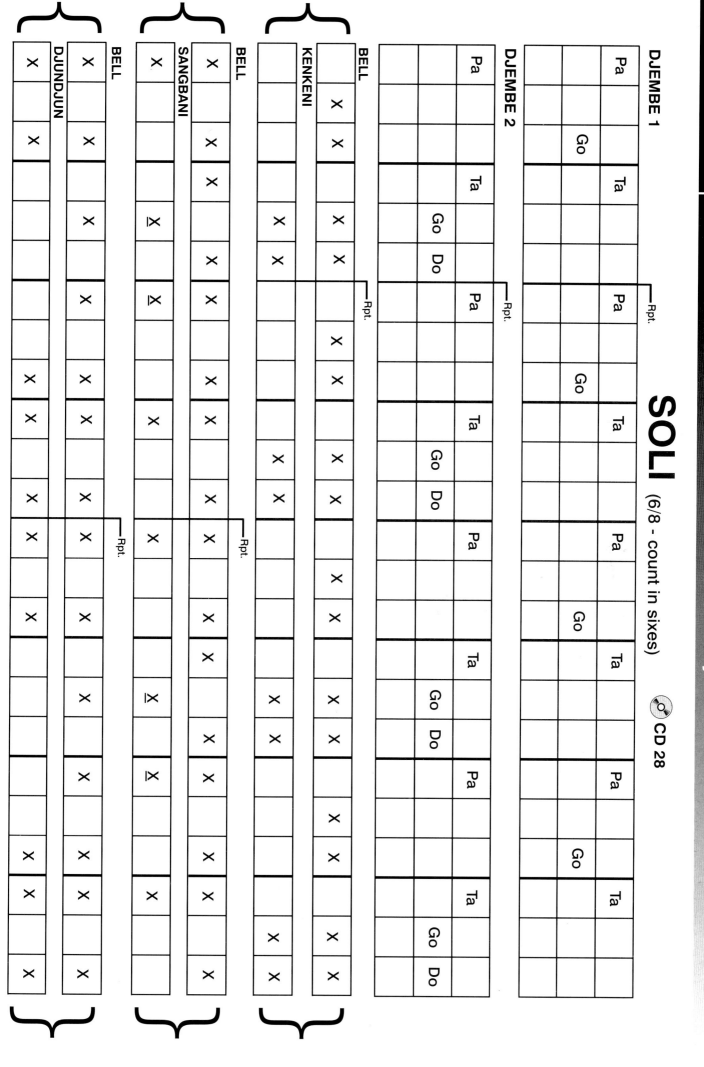

The skin is left to dry with the ropes hand-tight

# KASSA (6/8 count in sixes)  CD 29

**DJEMBE 1**

| Go | Do | Pa | Ta | | Pa | Ta | | Go | Do | Pa | Ta | | Gun | | Pa | Ta | | Pa | Ta | —Rpt. |
|----|----|----|----|----|----|----|----|----|----|----|----|----|----|----|----|----|----|----|----|----|

**DJEMBE 2**

| Pa | | Ta | Pa | | Go | Do | | Pa | | Gun | | Ta | Pa | | | Go | Do | —Rpt. |
|----|----|----|----|----|----|----|----|----|----|----|----|----|----|----|----|----|----|----|

**BELL**

| X | X | | X | | X | X | | X | | X | | X | X | | X | —Rpt. |
|---|---|---|---|---|---|---|---|---|---|---|---|---|---|---|---|---|

**KENKENI**

| X | X | X | | X | X | X | | X | | X̲ | —Rpt. |
|---|---|---|---|---|---|---|---|---|---|---|---|

**BELL**

| X | X | | X | | X | X | | X | | X | | X | X | | X | —Rpt. |
|---|---|---|---|---|---|---|---|---|---|---|---|---|---|---|---|---|

**SANGBANI**

| X | X | X | X̲ | | X | X̲ | | X | | X | —Rpt. |
|---|---|---|---|---|---|---|---|---|---|---|---|

**BELL**

| X̲ | | X | X̲ | | X̲ | | X | | X̲ | —Rpt. |
|----|---|---|----|---|----|---|---|---|----|---|

**DJUNDJUN**

| X | X | | X | | X | X | | X | | X | | X | X | | X | —Rpt. |
|---|---|---|---|---|---|---|---|---|---|---|---|---|---|---|---|---|

**BELL**

| X | X | X | | X | X | X | | X | | X | —Rpt. |
|---|---|---|---|---|---|---|---|---|---|---|---|

The fur on the skin is removed with a razor blade

# YANKADI (6/8 count in sixes)

CD 30

**DJEMBE 1**

| Gun | | | Ta | Pa | Dun | Go | Do | | Gun | | | Ta | Dun | Go | Do | | | Rpt. |
|-----|---|---|----|----|-----|----|----|---|-----|---|---|----|-----|----|----|---|---|------|

**DJEMBE 2**

| Pa | | Go | Do | | | Gdo | | Gdo | | | Pa | Ta | | | | | Rpt. |
|----|---|----|----|---|---|-----|---|-----|---|---|----|----|---|---|---|---|------|

**BELL**

| X̲ | X | X | X | X | X | X | | X | X | X | X | X | X | Rpt. |
|---|---|---|---|---|---|---|---|---|---|---|---|---|---|------|

**KENKENI**

| X̲ | X | X | X | X | X | X̲ | X | X | X | X | X | Rpt. |
|---|---|---|---|---|---|---|---|---|---|---|---|------|

**BELL**

| X | X | X | X | X | X | X | X̲ | X | X | X | X | Rpt. |
|---|---|---|---|---|---|---|---|---|---|---|---|------|

**SANGBANI**

| X | X | X | X | X | X | X | | X | X | X | X | X | Rpt. |
|---|---|---|---|---|---|---|---|---|---|---|---|---|------|

**BELL**

| X | X | X | X | X | X | X | | X | X | X | X | X | |
|---|---|---|---|---|---|---|---|---|---|---|---|---|---|

**DJUNDJUN**

| X | X | X | X | X | X | X | X | X | X | X | X | X |
|---|---|---|---|---|---|---|---|---|---|---|---|---|---|

When the skin is dry the rope is tightened with a lever

## CARABALI  (6/8 count in sixes)  ⊙ CD 31

### DJEMBE 1

| | Do | Go | Dun | Go | Do | Gun | Dun | | | Ta | Go | Do | Gun | Dun | Go | Do | Gun | Dun | Go | Do |
|---|---|---|---|---|---|---|---|---|---|---|---|---|---|---|---|---|---|---|---|---|

Gun — Rpt.

### DJEMBE 2

| Go | Go | Do | Go | Do | Go | Do | Gun | Do | Go | Dun | Go | Do | Gun | Do | Go | Dun | Go | Do | Gun | Do | Go | Dun |
|---|---|---|---|---|---|---|---|---|---|---|---|---|---|---|---|---|---|---|---|---|---|---|

Rpt.

### DJEMBE 3

| Pa | Pa | Ta | | Pa | Pa | | Pa | Pa | Ta | | Pa | Pa | | Pa | Pa | Ta | | Pa | Pa | Ta |
|---|---|---|---|---|---|---|---|---|---|---|---|---|---|---|---|---|---|---|---|---|

Rpt.

### BELL

| X | x | x | x | x | x | x | x | x | x |
|---|---|---|---|---|---|---|---|---|---|

Rpt.

### DJUNDJUN

| X | x | x | x | x | x | x |
|---|---|---|---|---|---|---|

### DJUNDJUN Continued

| X | x | x | x | x | x | x | x | x |
|---|---|---|---|---|---|---|---|---|

Rpt.

## Eight

Finally the skin is trimmed and the body oiled

Twelve West African Multi-Part Rhythms

# SOLO PLAYING & IMPROVISATION

The main ambition of many drummers is to become a skilled soloist and improvisational player.

I would hazard a guess and say that most beginners are first drawn to drumming by witnessing a skilled soloist in action, whether in an African style ensemble, a community group setting, or in one of the many forms of music which now use African, or African style drums.

Imagining yourself as a skilled artist is completely OK by me - I do it all the time - however, to actually become that artist is a long road, and a much more demanding one than many people imagine. Most people simply don't have the time on their hands to put in the continuous practice that it takes to become a soloist who can learn every drum part in the book, and still have the flair to play something different, which fits on top of the underlying rhythms and complements them rather than detracting from them.

I do not claim to be a skilled soloist, but in the course of writing this book, I've come across people who are, and in talking with them, certain pointers have arisen which can be used to develop your own skills.

**1) DEDICATION -** If you already have some other musical knowledge and skills, you may remember how it takes time to build them up, by studying, practicing, playing, making mistakes, studying, practicing, playing, making mistakes etc. etc. ad infinitum, until finally it comes right. Playing hand drums is no different to any other instrument in this respect. You have to expect the same amount of work and practice if you want to master the necessary skills.

**2) ABSORPTION -** allow yourself to be taught by as many people as possible, and absorb their teaching, their rhythms and their skills with an open mind. This can lead you in suprising directions, and bring knowledge to you that you didn't even know was there to be known !

**3) LISTENING -** As was once said by the leader of the Leeds School of Samba - *"You have to constantly immerse yourself in the rhythms !"*

You can do this by joining a group/circle, attending concerts and shows, if you're lucky enough to have them in your area, or listening to recordings (see appendix 3) if you can't get to live shows. Bear in mind that most recordings are of master players and world class groups, so you cannot expect to simply listen and immediately copy at their speed and skill level, but if you listen enough, parts of what you hear will stand out enough for you to remember and work on, if you have the basic skills.

**4) PRACTICE SLOW - LEARN QUICK -** This advice is often repeated in different forms, but it applies to almost every discipline you can think of, and it's no different in drumming. If you can't play it quickly, try playing it slowly, and through slow repetitions of a phrase or part, you can 'internalise' what you're doing, and it becomes ingrained in your natural neural pathways - i.e. it becomes 'second nature'. If you internalise lots of phrases which are not standard parts, and play them accurately, you'll be soloing ! Practice with your group and on your own, and practice every day, if you can.

No, practice every day, whether you can or not !

**5) STUDY THE RHYTHMS -** By studying rhythms you gain an understanding of what kind of phrases suit which kind of rhythms. Also by knowing the rhythms well, you will be able to pick out similarities and differences, and have a mental picture of, or feeling for, what is going on. When you have a good clear understanding of what IS going on, then you also, automatically, have the knowledge of what is NOT going on in that rhythm, and you can put something in, which is not already there !

A game which can be played with your group, is to build your own rhythm together, by each playing something simple which fits with, and adds to, what is already being played. Start with one player, and each add something simple which is not already there, until you have a living rhythm.

**6) KNOW YOUR CURRENT LIMITS, AND STRETCH THEM -** Begin as a soloist by playing short phrases which you have practiced and know well. Allow your confidence to build slowly, and you'll go further without embarrassing yourself. If you have a regular drumming group, you can arrange with them to have sessions in which you play support for each other whilst you practice soloing skills one at a time. In this way you can stretch your limits safely, and hopefully get feedback and share knowledge at the same time. Sometimes you might want to just bash it out a bit, and see how fast your hands will move, see if you can play twice the speed of the group. Other times, you might just want to try picking out interesting spaces in the rhythm already

being played, highlight the offbeat, or try playing a different count, and see what happens. Try rotating your own playing around the other part being played, copying, interjecting, answering phrases etc.

**7) PLAY WITH THE BASS DRUMS -** In chapter 3, I mentioned the theory that it is the djundjuns, not the djembes, which actually define the rhythm you are playing. This may be because within a particular rhythmic structure, e.g. 12/8 or 4/4, the djembe parts are, in effect interchangeable, but if you change the bass drum rhythm, you really aren't playing the same thing anymore. For instance, if you swap the bass line in Carabali, for the bass lines of Soli, you would be playing Soli, not Carabali, even if you didn't change the djembe parts. Thus, if your soloing fits in well with the bass drum parts, it will sound good, but if it contradicts or works against the bass drum parts, it can sound bad. At first, you can just try to put short sharp phrases into the gaps in the bass drum lines, and build up from there.

These seven points of advice all revolve around two main ideas -

The first is to listen, learn, and absorb with an open mind. Everybody has their own learning road - some start early in life, other start late, but paths cross all the time, and each crossing path is an opportunity for sharing and learning. The more you are looking, the more you will find, and you don't yet know where your drumming will take you, even if you know where you want to go.

The second is to take time to practice. Regular practice works best for most drummers, because it helps your brain to internalise new rhythms quickly. Practice slowly at first, and allow your body to wake up to a new rhythm. An old theatrical maxim has it that ;

*'Amateurs practice till they get it right - Professionals practice till they never get it wrong !*

As you absorb and practice more, you will discover links and cross references between rhythms and parts, which you can use, and build on, as a soloist. Soon you'll be able to put things in which weren't there before, but which fit perfectly, and at that point you'll suddenly get the freedom to really let fly.

# Part Four

Finding & Maintaining a Drum

# How to Choose an African Djembe

Once you have decided that you want to own an African djembe, you must learn to recognize a good drum from a poor one. This may mean putting aside some preconceptions and taking a look at the drums from a slightly different perspective than you might with other products. As mentioned previously, the vast majority of djembes from Africa are hand made, and most are made under what we might consider to be quite difficult conditions for manufacturing anything - never mind a musical instrument. It is important to be able to recognize a well made drum, first, and then to recognize when the <u>right</u> good drum has been found for <u>you</u> !

## SIGNS OF A WELL MADE DRUM

The first tendency of most people, when they are looking at drums in a shop, is to hit all the drums, and hear how they sound. Of course this is important, but a badly made drum can be made to sound good for a short time, simply by tuning it up - so beware of judging a drum solely on how it sounds in the shop, and look for the following signs of a good drum, in the body, rings, rope and skin.

## 1) A DECENT DRUM WILL HAVE A GOOD QUALITY BODY

Drums often develop cracks and fractures in transit from Africa due to poor handling or insufficient protection for the journey, and unless you have some woodworking skills, you may have to suffer a fracture developing until the drum becomes un-playable. Not <u>all</u> cracks are a problem, of course, some are merely cosmetic, but if you feel concerned, look for another drum. Whilst you are checking the body, look at the edge where your hands will strike (and which the drum skin is stretched over) - is it rounded, comfortable and smooth, as it should be, or is it square, uncomfortable, or jagged, which could hurt your hands or damage the skin ?

## 2) A DECENT DRUM WILL HAVE CLOTH-WRAPPED RINGS

The two metal rings which clamp the skin at the top, and the third ring near the waist of the drum should all be wrapped in cloth to prevent rust, and protect the skin and ropes from the iron. I don't know why the cloth prevents rust, but it does seem to work. You will only be able to see two of the three rings, but if <u>they</u> are not wrapped, forget that drum and look for another one. Unwrapped rings can lead to premature breakage of either the skin or the rope, and are best avoided.

Whilst you're checking the rings, make sure there are no signs of rust, and also look for protruding bits of welding at the join, which might damage the ropes or skin. Also, check that the rings fit quite close to the body of the drum. They should be quite snug to the wood. Make sure that the skin is clamped securely between the rings, and has not slipped out anywhere.

## 3) A DECENT DRUM WILL HAVE GOOD, STRONG ROPE

An average sized djembe is probably strung with 4mm or 5mm thick ropes. It need to be quite thick to take the strain and high tension of tuning. The best rope for a djembe is 8-braid to 16-braid, and should be pre-stretched. If the rope is simply twisted, rather than braided, look for another drum. Remember - the rope at the loops takes just as much tension as the rope in the verticals, and it's just as important for this rope to be good quality. Check that the loops are made from a similar quality rope, and check that all the rope is in good condition. Look out for undue fraying which could weaken the rope. Also check that knots are secure and nothing can come undone except the horizontal tuning rope.

Braided rope

Twisted rope

## 4) A DECENT DRUM WILL HAVE A DECENT SKIN

Drum skins are a bit like car tyres - they wear out with use and need to be replaced once in a while. If you were buying a car you would check the tyres were not old and worn out, and had no significant defects. So it is with your djembe skin - but how do you tell good from bad ? There is no consumer protection against defects here.

### DRUM SKIN DEFECTS

Some defects are quite easy to spot - rips in the skin on the playing surface are generally to be avoided, though some drums play perfectly well with minor pinholes in them. Any kind of 'long' tear, or scar mark should set alarm bells ringing, and some round holes can develop into tears under tension. The drum maker will have checked the skin for defects before it was put on the drum, but at that stage the hair on the skin may have hidden some faults, which would only show up when the hair was shaved off. When faults are found at that late stage, many makers would prefer not to start again with a new skin which might

just as likely have hidden faults, and I don't blame them one bit, but you as a buyer should be aware that faults can cause the skin to fail when it's tuned up.

### DRUM SKIN AGE

The age of the skin is hard to check. You can't just look to see if the tread is worn down like on a car tyre, but signs of age in a drum skin might include the following:

Worn away fur on the flaps at the outer edge- this might indicate that the drum has been played alot, and the player's hands have worn away the fur. Is the fur worn in a couple of clear places where the hands fell, or is it just patchy baldness?

Lots of diamond pattern Mali weave on the bowl of the drum- this might be attractive to look at, but it can indicate that a skin is old. It's difficult to tell if Mali weave has been put in over time, or if it is all fresh, but for you as the buyer, it is better to get a drum which is well tuned with the tension in the verticals, rather than from the weave, because you will need to add weave over the time that you own and play the drum, and if there's little or no room for you to do that, then life will be more complicated for you. (You can refer to the next chapter for more information about keeping your drum in tune, and about when to replace the skin) As a rule of thumb, one or two circuits of Mali weave is OK for a well tuned new drum. If there is already more than that, or if the drum does not sound right with that much weave, it may be best to check out other drums before buying.

## THINGS NOT TO WORRY ABOUT

Many African drums are not quite symmetrical or perfectly even in build. They may be a bit lop-sided as they stand on the floor. These things are just the result of being hand carved with rough hand tools, and are not to be worried about. Also don't worry too much if the skin and the bottom ring are a little bit lop-sided. It may be a good sign if they are nice and even, but it's no great problem if they aren't. Tiny hairline cracks in the body are usually no problem as long as they are not growing and you can see both ends of the crack. Avoid cracks which run from the base edge of the drum upwards, and those from the top edge downwards - and avoid drums with cracks in the bowl which leak air when the drum is struck. Defects in the skin which are outside the clamping rings will not affect your playing at all, but do check carefully where the skin goes over the edge of the body and is under tension, though not on the playing surface.

## OTHER THINGS TO CHECK IF YOU CAN

You can ask the seller of the drum where the drum came from. Refer to chapter 2 for information on African countries which make the best djembes. Try to buy from someone who plays the djembe, and knows what they are talking about. You may have to pay a little more, but it should be worth it in the longer term. This person is likely to know if the rope is pre-stretched, for example. Ask if they have a repair service, and a supply of African goat skins, and good rope, for replacement.
It may also be wise to check if the drum you are buying is of a suitable size for a case or bag of some sort. A good dealer will be able to help you here. They should also be able to refer you to a local drumming group or teacher. A drumming group may have drums that you can try out, so you can get more experience, and talk to some people who already own drums.

## GETTING THE RIGHT SIZE DRUM

It's important to find a drum which is not only of good quality, but also of the right size for you. This is often overlooked by novices, but the size of the drum in relation to your personal size will affect your playing a great deal.
The important thing to check is not the diameter of the drum head, but the overall height of the drum. The reason for this is that most of us do most of our playing in the seated position, and we need to find a drum where the playing surface is at the right height when we are sitting with the drum held between our knees, leaning away from us.

If you check chapter 4, you will remember that it's necessary to get a drum which stands tall enough for you when you play sitting down. If your drum is too low, the playing edge will sit too low between your knees, and your knees will impede your hands when you play.

If, on the other hand, your drum is taller than it needs to be, then you will find that you have to lift your shoulders to get your hands into most of the basic playing positions, and this would become tiring very quickly. If you are a djembe novice, the last thing you need is a drum which makes your shoulders tired unnecessarily - just drumming is quite tiring enough, thank you !

To test the height of a drum, ask the retailer for an average chair, and sit with the drum ready for playing. The base of the drum should rest on the floor, your feet should be flat on the floor, and the drum should be leaning away from you. In this position, the rim of the drum nearest to your body should be two or three inches above the flat of your upper thigh. See if you can reach all the basic stroke positions without pushing your wrists down between the drum and your legs, and without having to lift your shoulders ! Again, a good dealer should be able to help you find the right size drum.

# How To Tune An African Djembe

An African djembe is hand made, so you must allow for some differences and peculiarities in shape and construction - so don't worry if it is a little lopsided, or seems different from another drum in some small way.

The basic construction is the same for most drums of this type. There is a wooden body, a skin (usually goat or antelope) and three metal rings - two of which clamp the skin at the top of the drum, and the third, smaller ring at the waist. Most often this third ring is not removable. All three rings should be wrapped in cloth to stop them from rusting, or prevent any rust from getting to the skin.

You should only be able to see one of the two top rings - the other one will be covered by the skin.

Attached to the ring you can see is a series of loops of rope going around the drum head.

The same arrangement can be found at the bottom of the drum, except that the loops on the ring face up the drum instead of down it.

Between these two sets of loops, a third long rope goes up and down time and again, around the drum, until it meets itself where it started, and ties off through a loop. At this point there should be a couple of metres of spare on the end of the long 'verticals' rope.

This spare rope will be used to create the traditional diamond pattern by threading through the vertical ropes round and round the drum, in a way which pulls them first to one side and then the other, so pulling down on the rings at the top, and hence the skin.

## HOW TO CHANGE THE TUNING

The tuning is changed by any of three methods. The most common is to simply tap the visible ring at the top of the drum, gently with a hammer, all the way round the drum, so that the tension which is in the rope system is transferred over the edge into the skin. This tapping is often done in a rough way, but it makes sense to be as careful as possible, especially if you are inexperienced, as any damage to the skin can be very expensive in the long term.  It is best to use some kind of block which can be positioned on the ring and then hit with the hammer. Put the block onto the ring where there is some rope looping, so there is some cushioning for the metal ring. Make sure you use a block which does not have sharp edges which could cut the skin. As you move the block around the ring and tap it with the hammer, you should hear the tone of the drumskin rising bit by bit. If you don't hear this happening, you can either hit a bit harder with the hammer, or give up this method and move on to the ropework to tune your drum.

## HOW TO TUNE THE ROPES

There are two ways of adding tension to the ropes ; these are -

1) putting in more 'knots' - i.e. threading the loose end of the tuning rope further through the verticals to make more zigzags and diamonds

2) tightening up the vertical rope which goes up and down the drum between the rings/loops.

Of these two methods, the first is always to be tried first because it is the easiest, quickest and commonest, and it can be done quite confidently by a beginner. All you need is a medium screwdriver (to lift the ropes), something to grip the ropes with when pulling on it, and some time, patience and energy. Please take care to avoid back strain and blisters, as the rope tension can be quite high. Take your time, and if in doubt, call a more experienced person to help you or teach you.

fig. 1

### STAGE ONE- Identify the last 'knot'.

It may be necessary to undo a rope handle or otherwise untie the spare loose end of the rope from where it has been stored on the drum (often around the waist) before using it. Once this is done, you will be holding the loose rope and will be able to see where it emerges from the knotwork pattern.

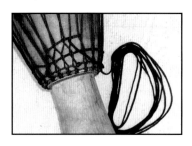

fig. 2

It should now be possible to see clearly if the rope is partway around the drum, or if it has completed a circle. If it is partway round, you will need to keep going in the same direction with your knots as the person who put in the existing knots, i.e. to the right, or to the left. If a circuit has

been completed, it should be tied off before starting again on a new circuit of knots in either direction.

### STAGE TWO - 'Feed under two'

You start the next knot by passing the end of the loose rope underneath two parts of the vertical rope.

Feed all the loose rope through and pull it down until it is level with or below the level of the other knots, (or as low as possible if it's a new circuit). ( It is important to keep the knot work low down so that more circuits can be fitted in above later on). It is easier to feed the rope through if you wedge a screwdriver under the vertical ropes first. Once all the loose rope is through, you can move on the stage two.

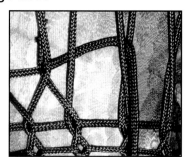

fig. 3

### STAGE TWO - 'Back under one'

You now have the loose rope wedged under two strands of the vertical rope, and you have the loose end in your hand. Pass it backwards so it goes back underneath the first of the two you went under.

fig. 4          fig. 5

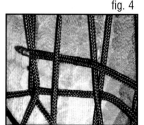 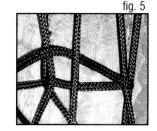

Now you can see how if you pull on the loose rope, the vertical strands will move towards each other. Move to stage three.

### STAGE THREE - 'Grip and pull'

You need to take a posture where you can pull hard on the rope whilst the drum stays where it is. You can squat on the drum and hold it down with your knees, or you can sit on a chair and hold it down with your feet. Either way, you must be careful not to strain yourself. For pulling the rope you can either use your hands and risk blisters, or wrap the rope around a stout stick (any teacher should be able to show you how) or use a cleat grip - this is a hand-held rope gripping device which is very quick and convenient to use. Either way, the technique is to pull the loose rope until the verticals cross over each other.

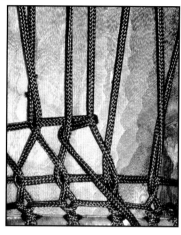

fig. 6

If the knot springs apart when you let go, you can form the first part of the next knot before pulling so that the rope is already trapped. It's usually OK to pull from that position.

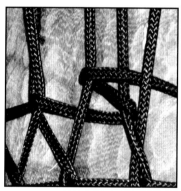

fig. 7

Beware of the temptation to continue putting in more and more knots without testing the sound of the drum by playing it. Tuning a drum is a bit like blowing up a balloon - with the balloon you want it to be as big as possible, and with the drum you want it to be as tight as possible, but the further you go, the greater is the chance of a burst skin. Always consult someone if you are worried.

If you have put lots of new knots in but your djembe is not sounding much better, or if you have run out of space to put more knots, you will have to try the second way of adding tension to the ropes. Be prepared for quite a lot of work

- this involves taking out all the existing knots before starting to tighten the vertical rope, and then putting knots back in for fine tuning afterwards.

## METHOD 2
### GETTING STARTED
Undo all the knots, round and round the drum. At this point some drums have been tied off at the point where one end of the rope goes through the loop on the other end, other drums are tied off at the loop on the bottom ring, and some are not tied off at all. It can be tightened either way, but I prefer to work with it loose.

You may like to gather around you the tools of the trade - i.e. a cleat grip (or pulling stick), a very small mole grips/clamping pliers, and a large-ish lever for exerting force on the ropes. Tightening can be achieved without these tools, but using the tools is the easier, blister free way to get good tension - I strongly recommend it.

Do bear in mind, as you go, that balloon mentioned above, and don't overdo it. It is far better to go around the drum several times tightening all the verticals a bit at a time, than to pull alot at any particular point on the skin. The aim must be to produce even tension around the drum, so take your time and don't strain yourself.

### THE FIRST FEW PULLS
First pull down on the vertical which is next to where the end loop is. This may pull the end loop up, but as long as it doesn't pop through the top ring loop, all will be well. Now pull any slack through the bottom ring loop into the next bit of vertical and then through the top ring loop into the third bit of vertical.
This is the next one to pull, as you will now be pulling on the skin again, and avoiding pulling on the bottom ring.
(Some tuners nail the bottom ring into position to prevent it getting out of position).
When you pull on this third bit of vertical, the first and second verticals are also affected, and in order to not lose the total

tension created, it's a good idea to clamp off (with your mini mole grips) at the top of the newly pulled vertical. This leaves you with slack rope in front of the clamp, and tight rope behind it.

Experience will show you where best to clamp - it's a good idea to get that experience now whilst the tension gained is not too great. *(see figures opposite)*

You must now work your way all around the drum repeating this process of pulling, clamping off, and feeding through, until you reach the end loop again. The last pull will tighten both ends of the rope at the same time, and you must now maintain the total tension by clamping on both ropes at the end loop whilst tying off by making a second pass under the ring loop at the bottom and hitching around the double rope you have created.

### NOW WHAT ?

Now you must decide whether to go around again (tuners who are not tired because they used the tools and took their time) or try to add any more tension by going back to knotting (tuners who are fed up and tired and have blistered hands). If the verticals are tight enough, you should be able to 'twang' them like bicycle spokes, and the skin should have a degree of tone which is not too far off decent. For more advice, consult with an expert.

### GETTING BACK TO KNOTS

So you have eventually tied off and want to fine tune using knots again - but which verticals should you cross first ? My rule of thumb is to start a new row by going under three verticals, and then ignore the

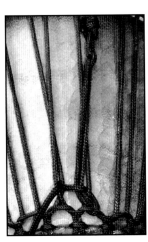

first when you make the knot, but it doesn't really matter, and by now you will have the confidence to backtrack if you don't like something you just did. It is important, however, to treat the double length of rope (which comes down from the end loop to the

fig. 12

bottom ring loop) as though it was a single vertical, and not to separate the two parts of it.

### HOW TO ATTACH A SHOULDER STRAP

A home made shoulder strap consists of a length of webbing or other material about 3.5 to 4 metres long, (depending on your height), and about 1" or 2" wide. You need to attach a little ring of rope around the waist of the drum, and another at the top - mine is tied onto the vertical rope at the top, but you could also attach it to the ring loop if you prefer. Now pass the strap material through both these rings and tie the ends of the strap together.

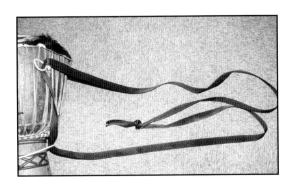

Now equalize the lengths of the two parts of the strap, and then cross the two equal halves like in the photo, and put your head through the double loop.

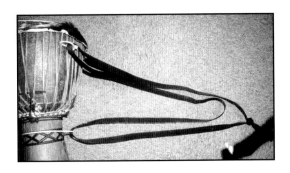

Now put your hands through between the straps on either side (this will be obvious when you do it) and follow through with your shoulders. Hey presto ! With some adjusting of the strap length for your height, you are now free to walk about wearing your drum.

fig.8. Pull on the vertical and clamp off.

fig. 9. Using a lever for extra tension.

fig. 10. Clamping off allows you to rest without losing rope tension.

fig. 11. Pull all the slack through the end loop and tie off. Note the use of a gripping cleat.

# How to Take Care of your Djembe

Now you have a djembe, it would be wise to get to know how best to look after it, so it will still be playing well in years to come.

## GET A CASE FOR YOUR DRUM

If you intend to move the drum about much from place to place, it would be best to invest in a case or bag which can protect the body, skin, and ropes all at the same time, and perhaps prevent your drum from damaging other items if it should roll or fall over.

Some cases are semi-hard plastic like drum kit cases, and for these you need to make sure you get a good fit for your individual drum, or add some internal padding/foam yourself. Some bags are simply made from cloth, and don't afford much protection to the drum. Others are mainly cloth, but have a padded cover for the drum skin built in. This is better, but the body of the drum is still vulnerable. The best cases I have seen are flexible coverall cases made from strong cordura nylon, with a fleecy style lining and overall padding built in. Consult your dealer for advice.

Whichever type of case you choose, make sure you get one which fits your drum nice and snug, or it will not give as much protection as it should. It's wise to check the carrying handles of the case or bag carefully - they must be strongly made to take the weight of the drum. Some cases have hand holds, other cases have shoulder straps, and some have both. Both is best, for carrying the case in different ways at different times. Remember to keep your drum in its case, for protection against impacts and falls, dirt, heat and cold.

## CARING FOR THE SKIN

New djembe owners often ask how best to care for the skin of their new drum, and the answer is more simple than they usually expect. The best thing you can do for a drum skin is to learn how to tune and de-tune it - tune it up for playing, and de-tune it for storage, even if only for a few days. Almost no-one actually bothers to do this, but it can more than double the life of your skin, because you are not keeping it at full tension the whole time. Re-skinning is a costly business (usually the price is about 1/3 the original price of the drum) so it makes sense to prolong the life of each skin as much as possible.

## TUNING & DE-TUNING

All you need to do is add or subtract up to half a dozen knots of Mali weave to tune or de-tune your drum. When you're used to it, this will only take a minute or two, and is especially easy if you carry in your case a couple of useful tools. These are 1) a medium screwdriver for lifting the ropes easily, and 2) a rope pulling device such as a clam cleat, a short stick, or even just a glove to protect the skin of your hand when you pull the rope. All the details of how to add knots of weave are in chapter 11, and if you are inexperienced, get someone to show you how easy it is, then make a habit of it, and it will quickly become second nature for you.

## RENOVATION WORKS

Apart from keeping the drum in a case, and caring for the skin, there is usually little to be done to your djembe when it's in one piece. Should you ever take it apart, for reskinning, for example, there are things which should be checked and if necessary altered, before putting it back together again.

Since there are only four main part to the drum - i.e. the body, the skin, the ropes, and the rings, it makes sense to examine each of these carefully, in turn, and renovate them if necessary.

There will never be a better time than now, and it would be foolish to put it all back together again with some part still needing attention. You can make your drum better by far, with just a little attention to detail at this stage.

## CHECKING THE BODY

The most important thing to check is the playing edge where your hands will strike - this should be made as smooth as possible, with the outer edges rounded over to give a comfortable playing surface. Ideally the surface should be level all the way round, without any bumps or cutaways - if the work is more than you can handle with a file and sandpaper, it might be worth consulting a woodworker friend who has some power tools.

Apart from renovating the playing edge, you should check the drum body for cracks which can be filled with woodworkers filler paste, (or with a mix of glue and wood-dust, which is the normal method in West Africa). Large cracks & fractures can be tackled with strong woodworker's glue and some binding tape. Again, if you lack the confidence or experience, you can consult a woodworker. The great beauty of wood as a material is that people have been working with it for thousands of years, and there's almost no fault that can't be fixed.

## CHECKING THE SKIN

All skins have marks on them. They are of animal origin, not from a plastics factory, and none of the them are completely blemish free, but having said that, skins should be checked for signs of stress, scars, holes and weak spots. This applies whether you are putting on a fresh skin, or putting back the old one. A pre-used skin will be easier to check, because it won't have any hair on it, and you may already be familiar with its individual marks, but  it may be a false economy to put it back on the drum, because the tensions on it will be different, and it must already have stretched compared to a fresh skin. I would advise always to put on a fresh skin unless you have no option.

To check a fresh skin, hold it up against a strong light, with the hairy side away from you, and look for signs of light coming through holes. Holes at the edges can be OK, because they can be kept off the playing area, but it is wise to mark them with a marker pen and then check that you have a large enough area - without holes - to effectively skin your drum. Apart from holes, check any scar tissue or any other area where light shines through more strongly than on the rest of the skin. Make sure there is nothing on either side of the skin such as dirt or blood etc. which would stop light coming through - these kind of materials can fool you by stopping the light which might otherwise shine through a hole or other defect.

## A NOTE ON RE-SKINNING

I believe that re-skinning is a task best shared by two people, and the best person to help you is someone with previous experience. Therefore, I'm not going to describe the re-skinning process in this book. There is an excellent video by Paulo Mattioli in the videography at the end, which shows a complete re-skin, re-rope, and tune up before your very eyes, and I highly recommend it if you intend to tackle the job without an experienced friend to help you.

## CHECKING THE ROPES

Poor rope is a real curse when it comes to re-tuning your drum, so check all the rope carefully.

If there are signs of fraying or near breakage do not use the same rope again. It is far easier to re-skin and tune-up with a fresh length of good quality rope you can trust, than to mess about with old frayed, knotted, or damaged rope. Remember that the ropes which form the loops on the tuning rings - both top and bottom - are just as important as the main length of rope, and must be of good quality and in good condition for effective tuning. Check out the video mentioned above for an illustration of how to replace the rope loops.

## CHECKING THE RINGS
It is a good idea to unwrap and check the rings as part of your renovation, even if you don't intend to do any metal work. The rings will be in close contact with the ropes and the skin, and if you can see any sharp edges or bits on the rings - particularly at or by the weld, you should at least take care to make sure they are covered by extra cloth in the re-wrapping process. Best of all would be to take a metal file to any such sharp edges - it may be fiddly, but it's not difficult.
When the drum is tuned, the ropes and skin will pull hard against the rings, and

remaining irregularities can cause fraying or breakage. When you are satisfied with the rings, re-wrap them in inch wide strips of cotton cloth (it doesn't have to be African, but nylon type cloths don't work so well, due to being slippery).
Weak or broken rings or welds need to be fixed by a welder who has TIG welding equipment.

Gas welding often just isn't strong enough for the tensions involved - and the last thing you want is for the weld to break again just as you're putting in the final tensioning after rebuilding your drum ! Do check when you take your rings for welding, and don't let a motor mechanic bluff you - people often underestimated the forces/tensions involved in a highly tuned djembe.

# Sources of Exercises & Rhythms

Basic system GunDun/Go do/Pa Ta - Nigerian. Babatunde Olatunji
As presented by Paulo Mattioli in the Hands on Drumming video tuition series. Paulo Mattioli himself credits Arthur Hull with the popularisation of this system throughout the USA, and Arthur Hull credits the inspirational Nigerian drummer Babatunde Olatunji.

## CHAPTER 5

| | |
|---|---|
| Exercises 1 to 11 | The author. |
| Exercise 12 | As taught by Guinean Master Musa Suma in Leeds. Passed to the author by Ivan Ratoyevsky. |
| Exercise 13 | common to many teachers and classes |
| Exercises 14 & 15 | Lamin Jassey - Leeds, England, 1997 |
| Exercise 16 | common exercise |

## CHAPTER 7

| | |
|---|---|
| Rhythm 1 | adapted by the author from a 'rhythm grid' copied from a school book. Author unknown. |
| Rhythm 2 | As presented by Brad Dutz on the instructional video 'Have fun playing hand drums - the djembe, Vol 2' |
| Rhythm 3 | adapted by the author from simple game, possibly first arranged by Jobina Pinkenburg. |
| Rhythm 4 | adapted by the author from Jim Griener's presentation on the tuition video 'Community Drumming'. |
| Rhythm 5 | Lamin Jassey - Leeds, England. 1997/8 |
| Rhythm 6 | adapted by the author - from Roger Wolfe, Leeds & Ilkley, England |
| Rhythm 7 | adapted by the author from Paulo Mattioli's arrangement. |
| Rhythm 8 | adapted by the author from 'Drumatrix' by Rosemary Schonfeld. |

## CHAPTER 8

| | |
|---|---|
| Kpanlogo | Ghanaian. Arr. Roger Wolfe |
| Gahu | Ghanaian. Arr. Jobina Pinkenburg - modified by the author |
| Afro-Cuban | Jim Greiner - modified by the author |
| Kuku | Jobina Pinkenburg |
| Kassagbe | Guinean. Arr. Paulo Mattioli |
| Gambian Song | Lamin Jassey |
| Fanti | Jobina Pinkenburg |
| Macrou | Guinean. Arr. Paulo Mattioli / Modified by the author |
| Soli | Guinean. Arr. Paulo Mattioli |
| Kassa | Guinean. Arr. Paulo Mattioli |
| Yankadi | Guinean. Arr. Paulo Mattioli |
| Carabali | Poss. Nigerian. Arr. Thomas Christen |

Transcriptions and presentation throughout by the author.

# Further study materials & resources

## Paulo Mattioli Djembe Tuition

### 'Hands-On Drumming' Series   (VIDEOS)

This will eventually be a series of six, but for now, there are four excellent teaching videos which show the various drum patterns for full ensemble playing using over shoulder filming, slow motion, hand on drum close ups etc. All include a recap of the three basic strokes.

Volume 1 YANKADI and MACROU

Volume 2 KASSAGBE and KASSA

Volume 3 SOLI and LIBERTE

Volume 4 TIRIBA and MINIANI

Volume 5 Not yet available

Volume 6 Not yet available

### West African Djembe Drumming   (VIDEO)

Paulo's first tuition video is less well produced than the Hands-On drumming series, but contains seven full rhythms in it's two hour presentation as well as the basic strokes and rhythm & technique exercises. The rhythms are Lamba, Doundounba, Lindjian, Sedeba, Aconcon, Koukou & Mandjiani.

### West African Djembe Drumming   (CASSETTE)

The 'pocket pal' of Mattioli tuition, this cassette provides reminders of the drum parts for eleven different rhythms - all the ones from the video above, plus Kakilambe, Temeni, Djong-dong & Wolosondon. They are presented part by part on side 1, and in ensemble on side 2. NB presentation is pretty rapid, with little repetition and no explanation of hand strokes.

### African Percussion - The Djembe  Serge Blanc

A highly regarded  intermediate/advanced level book and CD pack, recently translated from it's original French publication, this contains background information on West African Society and it's music, and contains 22 notated traditional Mandeng rhythms with complete audio examples, as well as introductory exercises for djembe, and for djembe with two djun-djuns. Uses Western musical staff notation throughout.

### Rhythms and Songs from Guinea Famadou Konate and Thomas Ott

Highly, highly recommended for both players and teachers. the combination of authors (Konate was lead djembe in Ballets Africains of Guinea for 36 years, whilst Ott is professor of music pedagogy at University of Cologne) has lead to a truly enlightening workbook for any djembe or African music enthusiast. Loads of chapters full of surprising and revealing information, with plenty of exercises and explanations leading to a deeper understanding of what makes African drumming sound so, well, 'African', and how yours can too.

### A Life for the Djembe-Traditional rhythms of the Malinke

Uschi Billmeier in conjunction with Mamady Keita - contains a wealth of information on life in old Guinea and the Malinke people in relation to their history and music. Gives the reader an ability to appreciate the notes about the cultural context of each rhythm. Not much basic instruction, but about 60 rhythms are presented in a fairly easy format developed by Billmeier, of which 21 are on the CD, with djembe and bass drum parts. Also gives contacts for the Tam Tam Mandingue school in Brussels , and for accredited teachers in other countries.

### Traditional Rhythms of the Mandingue-beginners
### Traditional Rhythms of the Mandingue-intermediates

Tuition videos by Manady Keita with a 6 strong percussion band, presenting seven full rhythms on the first tape, and eight on the second, more advanced tape. Although many of the rhythms are also presented in the tuition pack "A life for the djembe" (above) the advantage of the videos is that you see the master at play and the second tape contains soloing material - quite rare on a video.

### Djembefola- the latest djembe rhythms Daniel Genton

An advanced level book/CD pack in French and English , giving original and modern variations  of many (mainly Senegalese) rhythms. Best for players who read music and wish to expand their range and knowledge of rhythm variations.

### Le Djembe

Entirely written band presented in FRENCH, this must be the djembe owner's bible. An absolute wealth of information in over 200 A4 pages, with a 95 track CD.

**The above items available from your retailer,**
**or write to / email me for an up to date list.**

# Djembe resource guide

### Mandiani drum and Dance  Mark Sunkett
A high level book & CD pack which examines the West African djembe culture in some detail- it's history and traditions, it' drums and it's dances. Djembe build and design are looked at, and specific dance steps and rhythms are included. Rounding out the book are a critical analysis of the music and a fascinating comparison of African and African-American aesthetic views. 176pp

### The Healing Drum   Yaya Diallo
This book (with accompanying cassette) traces the author's extraordinary cultural legacy, exploring the Minianka view of the human being and the cosmos relative to daily work, celebration, medicine, dance, trance, initiation and death. In the tradition of Minianka, music is a remedy for both physical and psychological imbalances, harmonising the forces of the visible and invisible worlds. 213pp

### The Drummer's Path  Sule Greg Wilson
Book and cassette pack. This authentic and provocative introduction to African and Diaspora drumming provides a unique teaching tool for percussionists as well as a guide to the principles and power of traditional African rhythms for all dancers and drummers. Book 140pp Cassette contains rhythms, techniques, melodies and instruments from all over Africa, from India, South America, the Caribbean and US. One person's search for the root of spirit in music.

# Accessories, Spares and Repairs

### Djembe Bags
Protection Racket djembe bags come in 5 standard sizes (12", 13", 14", 15" & 16") and are the best value I've seen. Very heavy duty outer skin, chunky zip top, synthetic fleece lining, shoulder strap and hand grip. stronger than other bags up to twice the price.

### Djembe Stands
Branded djembe stands are designed around branded djembes, such as LP, Natal, Gibraltar, Toca, and Pulse, and design variations mean you should check that the stands will fit your drum and/or hold it just as you want it, at an angle you like.

### Djembe Straps    The Klondyke double shoulder strap
This new strap allows you to wear your drum in style, and unclip it whenever you want ! It features comfortable webbing, adjustable length, easy dog clip, and the straps cross over your back, so allowing your drum to hang securely right where you want it, with the weight being taken on both shoulders

### Skin it, tune it, play it   Paulo  Mattioli  (Video)
A complete re-skin and tune up before your very eyes - this film de-mystifies much, and examines the intricacies of djembe construction by taking one apart, putting it back together and tuning up to proper pitch- all the while explaining what to look out for and how to deal with what you find. Highly recommended

### Renovation, skins, rope etc
Most drum circles and many shops  offer a reskinning service, if you don't want to tackle it yourself. The supply of goat skins is irregular, though.

Good quality pre-stretched braided tuning rope is usually available by the metre or by the roll , from drum shops, yacht chandlers and outdoor shops. 35 metres will completely re-rope a djembe including the top and bottom hoops - 25 should be enough if the hoops are OK.  Smaller drums can get by with less.

### Tuning lever
For pulling proper tension into the vertical ropes you need some kind of lever. Many people use a big hammer handle, but now for the same price you can have this strong, purpose designed tuning lever which is 20" long with a slight taper to enable a quick release, and a deep step near the base to stop your rope from slipping when pulled.

### Cleat Grip
Blisters on your fingers ? The cleat grip is a real skin saver. Well known among boating enthusiasts and other rope users, the hand held cleat grip is an absolute must for pulling rope between 4mm and 6mm. Just slide the rope in from the side, lay it in the cleat, and pull ! The rope emerges from the centre of the grip, between your  middle fingers, so your hand and wrist remain straight. The cleat grip can be used at the end, or middle of the rope, for pulling or clamping knots or verticals.

**The above items available from your retailer,
or write to / email me for an up to date list.**

# List of Recordings

**Carabali** — **Rhythms from 'The Djembe Guide' CD**      (NTK 002CD)

Rhythms from this very book recorded live by my own band for your delectation. Includes Soli, Kuku, Fanti, Macrou, Yankadi, Carabali and Kassagbe. Cheap too!!

**Mystique d'Afrique** — **Master of the Forest**      CD      (AP 003)

High energy West African tribal dance rhythms from a one-off supergroup featuring Yamoussa Camara, Yamoussa Soumah, Mohamed Kemoko Sano, Brad Dutz, Abdoulaye Sylla, Sarah Abukutsa, Malang Bayo, Paulo Mattioli and Charmaine Renata Hubbard. These players represent between them the Ballet Djoliba, Les Ballets Africans, Les Merveilles D'Afrique, the Pan African Cultural Ensemble, and the National Dance Company of Senegal. There are twelve tracks here, many of which are taught in Paulo Mattioli's video tutors available in this catalogue.

| **Adama Drame** | — 30 years of Djembe | CD | (PS65177) |
| | — Mandingo Drums Volume 1 | CD | (PS65085) |
| | — Mandingo Drums Volume 2 | CD | (PS65122) |
| | — Giant of the Djembe | CD | (PS65211) |

"I was twelve years old in 1966 when I told my school master "Sir, I don't want to go to school anymore, I want to make music". Ever since that day I have thanked the good Lord for giving me the strength to have such a passion for music and for enabling me to play the jembe for the past thirty years and become it's ambassador all over the world." Though born in Burkina Faso, Adama Drame now lives in Ivory Coast. He is a master djembe player, the son, and grandson of a griot, and he regularly tours in both Africa and Europe.

| **Mamady Keita** | — Wassolon | CD | (FMD 159) |
| | — Nankama | CD | (FMD 195) |
| | — Hamanah | CD | (FMD 211) |
| | — Mogobalu | 2CD | (FMD 205) |
| | — Afo | CD | (FMD 215) |
| | — Balandugu Kan | 2CD | (FMD 218) |
| | — A Giate | CD | (FMD 224) |

Mamady Keita, from Wassolon, was chosen at the age of fourteen to play in the National Ballet Djoliba - he later became principal soloist and artistic director, and also worked with Souleymane Koli's Koteba troupe. Since 1988 he has lived in Europe, forming the famed percussion school Tam Tam Mandingue, and the ensemble Sewa Kan, and has taught throughout the continent, the USA and Japan. Wassolon and Nankama were recorded in Belgium with Sewa Kan, whilst Hamanah and the double CD Mogobalu were made back in Guinea after Keita returned to his home village in 1991 at age 41, and features many friends and teachers from his early years.

| **Various Artists** - Djembe : Percussions d'Afrique | CD | (82976-2) |
| — Djembe Volume 2 | CD | (82988-2) |
| — Djembe Volume 3 | CD | (82235-2) |

'Excellent samplers of (mainly Guinean) percussion, and percussion/dance ensembles, such as Ballets Africains, National Percssion Ensemble of Guinea, Wassa, Wofa, Famadou Konate and others. Much more than just djembe'.

| **Les Percussions de Guinea** - Volume 1 | CD | (82501-2) |
| — Volume 2 | CD | (92586-2) |

Stunning performances of traditional Guinean & other rhythms from this incredible seven man troupe playing djembe, doundounba (djun djun), segezege shakers, bote drum, taman (talking drum), fedounoun (calabash waterdrum), kirin (log drum),and the incredible plani bala (five headed djembe (!), with guest balafon players. Both volumes were recorded in theatre performance, but for volume 2 the audience was removed !

| **Famadou Konate** | — Hamana Foli Kan | CD | (82230-2) |
| | — Guinea-Malinke Rhythms & Songs | CD | (92727-2) |

Famadou Konate was born in Manina in the Hamana region of Guinea-one of the cradles of Malinke culture. Given his first djembe at at age two, he played in community ceremonies from age eight, and became renowned throughout the region.For twenty six years he was master drummer of the Guinea National Ballet, and he now plays in his own group 'Hamana Diara', and alongside Mamady Keita in the band "Mogobalu", He devotes much of his time to teaching in Africa and Europe, and his arrangements are supremely accessible , melodic, and inspiring.